Lake District
Eastern Fells

Dalesman Publishing Company
Stable Courtyard, Broughton Hall,
Skipton, North Yorkshire BD23 3AE

First Edition 1998

Text © Paddy Dillon 1998
Maps by Jeremy Ashcroft
Cover photograph: Grisedale Tarn from Seat
Sandal by Phil Woolley

A British Library Cataloguing in Publication
record is available for this book

ISBN 185568 123 4

Printed by Midas Printing (HK) Ltd

Lake District
Eastern Fells

Paddy Dillon

Companion volume to Lake District
Western Fells by Paddy Dillon

Series editor Terry Marsh

DALESMAN

Eastern Fells

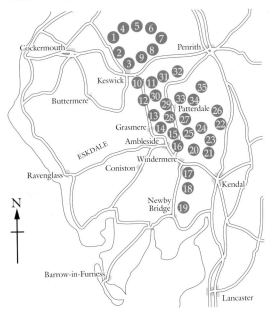

Contents

INTRODUCTION

All the walks in this book lie to the east of a line that runs from Bassenthwaite Lake, through Keswick, past Thirlmere, over Dunmail Raise, past Grasmere to Ambleside, and finally along the length of Windermere. The walks are immensely varied, from high fells to lake shores. There are mountain walks, hill walks, moorland walks, forest walks, riverside walks and walks which pass through fields, villages and towns. Together they offer an insight into the landscape of the Lake District, its life, work and traditions. Museums and visitor centres are mentioned where they occur, as well as other visitor facilities.

Geology

The ancient Ordovician bedrocks of the Lake District are the poor quality Skiddaw Slates, which form the friable screes covering much of the northern and north-western fells, as well as the area around Black Combe in the south. Most of the central parts of Lakeland are formed of the Borrowdale Volcanic series – massive beds of ill-sorted ashes and lavas which break into large blocks of rock and weather into very rough textures. To the south, around Coniston and Windermere, a succession of Silurian grits, slates, flags and limestone can be traced. In the western half of the Lake District there are massive intrusions of granitic rocks, notably in Eskdale and Ennerdale, with less prominent intrusions around the Skiddaw Fells in the north and the Shap Fells in the east. These intrusions often brought streams of mineral-rich fluids and vapours into the surrounding rocks. The whole fringe of the Lake District is surrounded by Carboniferous limestone bands, as well as by coal measures, sandstones, shales and grits. Despite the varied layers of rock, the fundamental shape of the Lake District was determined in the Ice Age, a relatively recent period, when massive glaciers widened and deepened existing valleys and scoured out the deep troughs which now hold the lakes and tarns. Hummocky masses of moraine can be distinguished in many places, as well as ice-scoured humps of rock.

History

In the Bronze Age the western half of the Lake District was well settled and aerial photographs reveal a number of sites featuring cairns, monuments and hut circles. The Romans are known to have penetrated the Lake District from Penrith to Ravenglass, and a string of their forts can still be inspected, along with traces of their roads. Following the departure of the Romans, the Dark Ages really do seem to have been dark in Lakeland, and there are few references to the region until the 12th century, although Norse placenames were certainly imposed before that time. The Normans came late into Cumbria and close on their heels came the establishment of monastic estates. It was from those times that large scale grazing became established and continues to be important. Family farming with secure tenure dates from the 16th century and the farmers were known as "statesmen". Agricultural improvements and enclosures with drystone walls helped to tame the appearance of the lower lands, leaving only the towering fells in a wild state. Mining and quarrying became more and more important, but the only real large scale developments occurred on the fringes of Lakeland. The activities of the "Lake Poets" paved the way for tourism, increased road transport, railways, the building of hotels and lodging houses.

Natural History

Originally, the Lake District was clothed in dense forest with only the highest peaks protruding above the trees. Lake margins were tangled with vegetation or featured areas of marshy ground. Despite its wilderness appearance today, the Lakeland fells have been well and truly tamed. Centuries of sheep grazing have prevented the tree cover from re-establishing itself, led to a decrease in plant species and contributed to erosion. The flora of the fells is remarkably different from what preceded it. Wiry grasses and heathers cover places where forests once grew, and only in a few places do stunted sessile oaks cling to rocky faces to remind visitors of those times. Unstable screes and other rocky areas are often profusely covered by clumps of parsley fern, and this pioneer plant binds loose ground so that other species can gain a roothold.

All the peat seen on the broader fells and moorlands is made up of decayed plant remains and sometimes the roots and bark of long-dead trees can be distinguished. Tree cover is being re-established, unfortunately with alien conifers in many instances, while introduced rhododendrons run riot in other areas. As sheep graze back the grass cover, invasive bracken colonises whole fellsides and proves useless for man and beast.

While a few species of deer are found in the Lake District, their presence in forests is a nuisance and they are likely to be shot. Foxes and badgers take their chances, and there are many packs of foxhounds loosed on the fells to be followed on foot by their masters. Red squirrels have one of their last strongholds in the Lake District, but creatures such as the pine marten are barely holding on to existence. Bird life is profuse, and many passage migrants can be spotted as they cross the narrow parts of northern England. The abundance of water attracts every kind of water fowl, and the proximity of the coast ensures that species of gulls and waders are commonplace even on the high fells.

Weather

Lakeland weather is at best unpredictable. Whatever the national weather forecasts may claim, mountainous areas generate their own brand of weather. Summers can be hot, but are not necessarily always hot. Likewise, winters can be cold, but sometimes weeks can pass without any snow cover. In between, almost anything could happen. In a particularly harsh winter, the fells can be truly arctic and no-one should venture into them unprepared. This can mean dressing in warm protective clothing and carrying full bivouac kit, as well as ice axe and crampons. In high summer, clear skies can cause intense heat and a combined danger of sunstroke and sunburn. This time, cool protective clothing, a hat with good shade, plenty of suncream and plenty to drink are required.

Traditionally, walking in the Lake District conjures up memories of rain and mist, which is perhaps unfair, but often true. Waterproofs, spare dry clothes, and an alertness to the dangers of cold and hyperthermia are required. In mist, the ability to navigate carefully and accurately with a map and compass is essential.

Felltop weather forecasts can be obtained which are specifically drafted to take account of Lake District conditions. Weather notices are often posted at information centres and some car parks, and it is also possible to telephone and take notes from a recorded weather announcement on (017687) 75757 or (0891) 500419.

Advice to Walkers

Walking is all about putting one foot in front of another. Walking safely means watching where you are putting those feet. The best advice is to tackle routes which are within your capabilities, and to turn back if you feel that you are in danger of exceeding your capabilities. Accidents generally happen when people don't take care about where they are heading, or try to do something which is beyond their capabilities. Accidents are best avoided altogether by knowing what can go wrong and taking steps to ensure it doesn't go wrong. Minor cuts and grazes will be sustained at some point, so a basic first aid kit should be carried. Adding further items to take care of more serious trouble is a good idea. You may not need them yourself, but someone else might.

If the worst comes to the worst and there is a serious accident needing professional help, then there are courses of action to be followed. If you are walking alone, then you are on your own and need to summon help from anyone who might be passing. This is generally done by blowing the International Mountain Distress Signal from a whistle. If you have companions, then some can stay with you while others go for help. Help is readily summoned from the nearest telephone, or from a mobile phone, by dialling 999 and asking for the Mountain Rescue. At this point let the experts take over and do exactly as you are told.

Access

Throughout England and Wales, access comes in many guises. There are public rights of way which include footpaths, bridleways and byways. There are also permitted paths and access areas, where there may be occasional restrictions on use. In the Lake District, there is a long tradition of virtual free access to the fells. This freedom comes with immense responsibilities and there must never be any abuse of it. All the land in the Lake District is owned by someone. Walkers have a right of passage across that land when they are following rights of way. Walkers are allowed on to permitted paths and access areas, subject to any restrictions that might be in force. The presence of walkers on most of the rugged fell tops and fellsides has long been accepted, but is not a right. There is no right to pitch a tent anywhere without permission, though in many secluded places on the high fells an overnight pitch will be tolerated provided that no damage or litter is caused. It is in the interests of all walkers to be extremely respectful of all the land they cross, and to be friendly and polite to those whose land and livelihood it is.

Maps

Choosing maps is worth a moment of thought. A map covering the whole of the Lake District on a single sheet is likely to be too simple or too cluttered with detail for it to be of any great use. The Ordnance Survey produce useful maps at scales of 1:50,000 and 1:25,000. The 1:50,000 maps are known as Landranger Maps, and the Lake District is covered by sheets 89, 90, 96 and 97. The 1:25,000 maps are known as Outdoor Leisure Maps and the Lake District is covered by sheets 4, 5, 6 and 7. This does not offer complete coverage of the area, and some peripheral parts need to be supplemented by 1:25,000 scale Pathfinder Maps.

Another important publisher of maps is Harvey Map Services. Harvey's produce extremely detailed maps giving a very clear picture of the landscape at scales of 1:40,000 and 1:25,000. The 1:40,000 maps are known as The Walker's Map, while the 1:25,000 maps are known as Superwalkers. Titles in both series include

Northern, North-Western, Western, Southern, Central and Eastern, but they don't quite cover all the walks in this book. They come complete with Visitor Guides offering background details to the area, ideas for walks and other information. Harvey's maps are all waterproof, while Ordnance Survey maps can be bought in waterproof laminates if required.

Distances and Height Gain

The walks in this guidebook range from 5 to 15 miles (8 to 24km). Average walkers will not have any difficulty completing any of them in a day, and many may be completed in a morning or an afternoon. It is important not only to look at the distance, but also at the height gain. The height gain can be as little as 330ft/100m, or as great as 3,500ft/1,050m. A combination of the distance and the height gain can give some idea of the time needed to complete any particular walk, but the nature of the terrain is also important.

Individual approaches to walking cause even more variation – lengthy lunch breaks, frequent stops to admire the view, or lengthy discussions with companions. The time allowance is merely a guide and should be adjusted in the light of individual performance. It generally refers to the time needed to complete the walk without too much hurry, but without any allowance for stops along the way.

Getting There

In past centuries, few would have risked venturing

to the Lake District, but in modern times road and rail transport make the journey easy and straightforward. Although the rail network has been reduced from its former glory, visitors can still reach Penrith, Kendal, Windermere, Grange-over-Sands, Ulverston, and all points along the West Cumbria Coast. There are National Express coach services into the Lake District, serving places such as Kendal, Windermere and Keswick. Travelling to the area by car is facilitated by good motorway and main road approaches, but there is a danger of grinding to a halt at Lakeland bottlenecks in peak periods.

Getting Around

Once inside the Lake District, most of the bus services are operated by Cumberland, which is part of the Stagecoach Group. There are also important Post Bus services to some remote parts, while the Ravenglass & Eskdale Railway provides a novel route through Eskdale. In some areas, Lake steamer services could be used to join or leave a particular walk. Full details of all public transport options within the Lake District can be obtained from a helpline number (01228) 606000.

Some of the larger car parks around the Lake District make heavy charges for parking, while many of the smaller car parks can quickly become crowded. Unsightly double yellow lines have been applied to miles of rural roads to deter inconsiderate roadside parking. Carelessly parked cars have resulted in traffic jams and consequent delays to public transport and emergency services.

Visiting walkers should consider leaving their cars at home and using the public transport network.

Where to Stay

There is abundant accommodation in the Lake District, from campsites to bunkhouses, Youth Hostels, B&Bs and hotels, not to mention self-catering cottages and caravans. Wise walkers will book their beds in advance and enquire about local facilities. If searching for accommodation at the last minute, the best plan is to go to one of the Tourist Information Centres and see if they can ring around and book a bed. They will often do this for a set fee or a percentage of the booking fee. With more time to plan ahead, there are all sorts of handbooks and brochures listing accommodation.

Tourist Information

Tourist Information Centres are usually provided by local authorities, while National Park Centres are provided by the National Park Authority. Generally, it is the Tourist Information Centres which are best able to handle accommodation bookings and provide visitors with coverage of facilities, and things to do and see. The National Park Centres are better able to supply details relating to conservation, wildlife, etc.

KESWICK

Keswick is the Lake District's major town, nestling in a verdant vale with fine fells on all sides. Its main street is dominated by the Moot Hall, which houses the Tourist Information Centre. Outdoor gear and craft shops abound, along with pubs, restaurants and cafes. There is a full range of accommodation from camp sites to large hotels.

This book covers half of the Lake District and as the dividing line runs through Keswick, only walks to the north of the town are described. There are three walks in this section, spread across the broad and sprawling slopes of the Skiddaw fells. Skiddaw is Keswick's mountain, dominating the town even when seen from the bustling main street.

There is a fairly quiet way of reaching the summit of Skiddaw, and this is the first walk to be described, taking in a circuit around Southerndale

Christine Isherwood

Skiddaw and Derwent Water

and Dash Falls. The second walk is the more usual ascent to the lofty summit, with a bit of variety introduced by descending steeply to Millbeck afterwards. The final walk hugs the slopes of Skiddaw and neighbouring Blencathra, exploring the Glenderaterra Valley and the Keswick Railway Path. Views from the top of Skiddaw in clear weather on the first two walks can be extensive, while the true nature of the sprawling slopes of the fells can be appreciated from the third walk.

Skiddaw is a natural focus of attention for walkers based in Keswick, but from the top of the fell the eye is drawn to the bleak, rolling moorlands termed as the "Back o'Skidda". While Keswick may have a full range of facilities, the countryside around Skiddaw is mostly lacking in facilities. There is the simple shepherds' dwelling of Skiddaw House, which has been converted into a Youth Hostel. While Skiddaw House makes a good base for hostellers wishing to explore the "Back o'Skidda", it is important to carry practically all the supplies which might be needed as the hostel stocks only a limited range of provisions.

Keswick is the terminus for a number of bus services. There are all year round services towards Penrith, Cockermouth, Ambleside and Borrowdale, with summer services running across Whinlatter Pass to reach Buttermere. By using bus services and taking careful note of their running times, walks need not always be circular, but can be extended across whole ranges of fells to link with an appropriate service back to Keswick.

1 Skiddaw from Southerndale

Skiddaw is one of the highest fells in the Lake District and it dominates the bustling town of Keswick. There are some mean fellwalkers who delight in referring to Skiddaw as a "slag heap" but they are outnumbered by those who have a high regard for the mountain. While it is true that there are some steep slopes of broken slate which unfortunately resemble quarry spoil, there are also approaches which limit crossing that sort of terrain. Climb Skiddaw from Southerndale to enjoy a rugged ridge, a quiet ascent, and a dramatic descent beside Dash Falls.

Distance: 8 miles/13km	*fellwalking, but with steep ascents and descents.*
Height gain: 2,625ft/800m	**Start/Finish:** *High Side, near Bassenthwaite.*
Walking time: 5 hours	*GR236311.*
Type of walk: *Simple*	

The route starts at High Side, not far from the village of Bassenthwaite. There is a small space where cars can be parked beside the road and there is a signpost pointing into the fields beyond. Walkers arriving by bus on the main road have only to walk a short way up the minor road at High Side to find the start of the walk.

Follow the route which is waymarked through the lower fields, zigzagging uphill alongside walls and hedgerows. The arrows point the way on to the open fellside beyond, where the route leads up to the foot of Ullock Pike. The slope steepens by degrees, but there are level stances along the way where it is possible to pause comfortably and enjoy the wonderful unfolding views across Bassenthwaite Lake and the Vale of Keswick.

Although Ullock Pike appears to be a pointed peak of rock, it is only the blunt end of a long, narrow ridge which continues towards Long Side and Carl Side.

The walk over Long Side and Carl Side is accomplished easily at around 2,300ft/700m on a well trodden path. The most obvious trodden path narrowly misses the true summit of Carl Side and swings left on to the steep slopes of Skiddaw. Loose, slaty material needs a little care, but the path is clear and should simply be followed ever upwards. Views back across Keswick and Derwent Water, to the fells surrounding Borrowdale, are enchanting.

The high crest of Skiddaw features three distinct bumps, the final one bearing the summit trig point at 3,054ft/931m. Extensive views in clear weather take in practically all of the most prominent Lakeland Fells, a good stretch of the Pennines and substantial areas of southern Scotland. Walkers unfamiliar with the country "Back o'Skidda" will note its rolling, wilderness moorlands, but even this once quiet corner is now becoming busier.

Continue by following a path roughly northwards to start the descent from the summit, picking a way

down another steep slope of broken slate. A fence later acts as a guide down the steep slope, levelling out for a short stretch on the minor hump of Bakestall. A steeper, grassy slope drops further downhill and the fence keeps walkers well clear of the dark cliffs of Dead Crags. A short length of drystone wall finally leads down to a fine track at the bottom of the slope.

Turn left to follow the rough track around the northern flanks of Skiddaw. In the other direction, it runs to the lonely Skiddaw House Youth Hostel. Just off the course of the track are the Dash Falls, also known as Whitewater Dash. There is one stance overlooking a fine fall, but other parts of the falls are seen only from distant viewpoints. Follow the track further downhill, enjoying the rocky surroundings and steep slopes of heather and bilberry. Cross a bridge and pass through a gate, then continue along the lower stretch of the track, which is surfaced with tarmac. A small parking space and a minor road are reached near Peter House Farm.

Turn left along the minor road and follow it downhill to cross Walk Mill Bridge. The road then climbs slightly and runs back to the small parking space where the walk started.

2 Skiddaw from Keswick

Skiddaw looms large over Keswick and its slopes soar skywards in colours that vary through the seasons as grass, heather and bracken constantly change their hues. Some walkers will start the ascent from Keswick, but motorists can get a bit of a leg-up towards Skiddaw by driving to the Latrigg car park. The steep ascent is a classic climb, which in the past was completed by tourists riding ponies. The descent from Skiddaw to Millbeck is steeper and should be taken slowly and steadily.

Distance: 7¼ miles/12km
Height gain: 2,660ft/810m
Walking time: 4 hours
Type of walk: Simple fellwalking, but includes some long and steep sections.
Start/Finish: Latrigg car park. GR281254.

Cars can be driven from Keswick to Latrigg by following minor roads through Ormathwaite. The final climb ends suddenly at a car park in between Latrigg and the broad slopes of Skiddaw. Walkers without cars can climb up the slopes of Latrigg to reach the car park and should refer to the route description in the next chapter. An obvious path seems to head more towards Blencathra than Skiddaw, but it quickly turns left and passes a cross

raised in memory of three shepherds. The initial ascent is gentle, climbing alongside a fence, but ahead the slope is much steeper.

Some walkers think the climb is tedious, noting only the change from bracken to heather to grass on the broad slopes. In clear weather, however, it is worth pausing to examine the ever expanding view across the Vale of Keswick and Derwent Water.

The line of the fence gives way to the line of a wall, then the clear path pulls away from the wall and the twin summits of Skiddaw Little Man are seen ahead. The walking is easier as the gradient is gentler. Skiddaw's summit is seen as the path passes another fence. There is an option at this point to keep to the left and climb over the top of Skiddaw Little Man as an extra.

Skiddaw's final slopes are steep and covered in loose slate, but this last climb is not too difficult and the airy summit ridge is soon gained.

There are three broad swellings on this ridge, with the furthermost one bearing the summit trig point at 3,054ft/931m. In clear weather the view encompasses practically all of the most prominent Lakeland Fells. Looking northwards takes in great tracts of southern Scotland, while westwards are the North Pennines. The country close to hand is known as the "Back o'Skidda" and is composed of rolling, wilderness moorlands and hills.

Retrace steps back along the summit crest, but don't be drawn off to the left along the path used for the ascent. Instead, look out for another path leading off south-westwards towards Carl Side. This path is steep and covered in loose slaty scree, but it cuts a clear line across the slope and is fine to follow if taken steadily. There is a grand view along the length of Southerndale. In mist, take care on the broad summit of Carl Side as there are a number of paths which could lead to confusion.

Cross over the grassy hump of Carl Side and aim to pick up a path running southwards, as if towards Derwent Water. The grassy slopes steepen considerably, and the descent crosses a rocky area at White Stones. Enjoy the fine views forwards, as they gradually pass from sight on the way downhill. The path zigzags past White Stones and continues down rugged slopes to Doups. After crossing a fence on the lower part of the slope, turn right along another path to reach a minor road at Millbeck.

Turn left to follow the minor road through Millbeck, and keep left at any other road junctions to pass through Applethwaite and climb back up towards the Latrigg car park. The road from Underscar to the car park will have been driven along earlier in the day. Walkers who have no need to return to the Latrigg car park could follow roads from Millbeck to Keswick. There are only a couple of options for avoiding the road walk back into town, as there are no direct footpath links.

3 Glenderaterra

Skiddaw and Blencathra are separated by the deeply cut cleft of the Glenderaterra Valley. So complete is the severance of these two mighty fells that there are few walkers who would even dream of linking them in a day's walk. The Glenderaterra Beck drains a boggy moorland bowl behind Skiddaw and Blencathra, bringing water from the fells to augment the flow of the lovely River Greta. This walk explores both sides of the Glenderaterra Valley and concludes with a stroll along the Keswick Railway Path.

Distance: 9 miles/15.5km **Height gain:** 1,300ft/400m **Walking time:** 5 hours	**Type of walk:** Simple low level fellwalking on good tracks and paths. **Start/Finish:** Keswick Leisure Pool. GR270238.

The Keswick Leisure Pool has been constructed on the trackbed of the Cockermouth, Keswick & Penrith Railway, which will be followed towards the end of the walk. To start the walk, head back along Brundholme Road and turn right on to Spooney Green Lane. A bridge takes the lane across the busy A66 road and a farmhouse is passed. The track continues up the forested slopes of Latrigg, where the clearest line leads to the Latrigg car park.

Leave the car park by following a clear path which seems to head towards Blencathra. It quickly turns left and faces the steep slopes of Skiddaw. Do not follow the path running straight uphill alongside a fence, but bear slightly to the right and follow another path which crosses Whit Beck. The valley enclosing the beck is covered in bracken and the track is part of the Cumbria Way.

Follow the track as it contours around the lower slopes of Lonscale Fell. There is a slight ascent, but the line is well trodden and keeps walkers clear of rugged ground. The track gradually bends to the left as it enters the confines of the Glenderaterra Valley. There are steep and rocky slopes above and below, but the path is easy to follow and presents no problems for walkers. There is a slight ascent, followed by a slight descent, as the path pushes further into the valley. The fell of Great Calva stands in a prominent position on the far skyline.

Look out for a turning to the right towards the head of the valley, where another clear path drops downhill, passes through a gate, and uses footbridges to cross a couple of becks. Walkers are transferred from one side of the Glenderaterra Valley to the other, and looking back Lonscale Fell adopts truly Alpine lines. Heading southwards through the valley, a fine track rises gently across the slopes of Blease Fell, a shoulder of Blencathra. This track leads unerringly through the valley, emerging on to the front slopes of the fell and reaching a road near the Blencathra Centre.

A cattle grid and gateway are reached at the

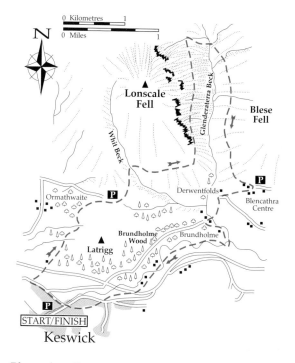

Blencathra Centre, and there is a footpath sign on the right. Follow this and further waymark arrows through the buildings which make up the Blencathra Centre, continuing down through fields towards the farm called Derwentfolds. Turn left at Derwentfolds to follow another path down into a wooded river valley. Cross the river using the footbridge provided, then turn left to take a minor road downhill passing Brundholme Farm.

Look out for a gateway on the right which gives

direct access to the line of the Keswick Railway Path. The old trackbed of the Cockermouth, Keswick & Penrith Railway has been made available as a walkway leading back to Keswick. Simply turn right to follow it. There is an old railway navvy hut nearby which offers shelter from inclement weather and also contains interesting historical notes about the old railway and the surrounding area.

Although the railway tracks were lifted after the closure of the line in 1972, the impressive "bowstring" girderwork bridges were retained. The railway path uses a handful of bridges as it crosses and recrosses the River Greta in its wooded valley. The Brundholme Woods are predominantly oak, while later views between the trees reveal the sites of old mills at Brigham. The mills had a varied working life and produced bobbins, pencils, cotton, wool, soya and even electricity.

The busy A66 road soars across the River Greta and the old railway at Brigham, and there is a temporary interruption to the line of the trackbed. Follow steps up and down to regain the course of the old line. The Keswick Railway Path cuts straight through the suburbs of Keswick, passing the site of the town's railway station before ending back at the Keswick Leisure Pool.

CALDBECK

An old saying relates that "Caldbeck Fells are worth all England else", and walkers might be wondering why local folk seem so patriotic about this particular patch of countryside. The answer lies deep underground, where there is an amazing mineral wealth that was long exploited. There are two rock types which come into contact in these parts, granite and gabbro. The mineral structure of these two rock types is radically different and for them to come into contact is rare. Hot fluids and vapours were pushed into the surrounding rocks by both of these igneous intrusions, leaving behind an amazing array of minerals. There are compounds found beneath the Caldbeck Fells which are found nowhere else in Britain. Evidence of mining activites will be encountered from time to time on these fells, so it is important to keep clear of any old shafts and levels.

The kestrel in flight

Christine Isherwood

There are three walks in this area, including both the Uldale Fells and Caldbeck Fells. One walk traverses the broad moorland slopes of Great Sca Fell, which is not to be confused with the famous Scafells of western Lakeland. Nor will there be the attendant crowds which are a feature of those higher fells. High Pike is crossed on another walk and can be regarded as the northernmost summit of the Lake District before the plains of Carlisle.

Consequently, views can be extensive from the summit.

The final walk is over the rugged Carrock Fell. This is where most of the gabbro outcrops and the fell is noticeably more rugged than others in the area.

Walking in the Caldbeck Fells is to walk off the beaten track. Other walkers are beginning to explore the area, but essentially this is a quiet tract of countryside with few facilities. There are a number of small villages, but not all of them can offer food, drink or accommodation. Caldbeck offers more than most, but it is well to the north. Public transport is virtually absent in the area. The Carrock Fell Youth Hostel offers a base for walkers and there are farmhouse B&Bs in the countryside.

The course of the Cumbria Way can be traced in places. The route has a high and low level option as it crosses these fells. Leaving Keswick, the route heads through the Glenderaterra Valley to Skiddaw House Youth Hostel. One branch heads for Dash Falls and takes low level tracks and minor roads to Caldbeck. The other branch heads for the River Caldew, then climbs over High Pike before descending to Caldbeck. The Cumbria Way has introduced many walkers to the quiet pleasures of these rounded hills after the bustle of the big fells to the south.

4 Great Sca Fell

Most walkers in the Lake District could reach for their maps and proudly indicate the whereabouts of Scafell and Scafell Pike. They would be less sure about Great Sca Fell, which is an unremarkable hump of grass tucked away in a quiet corner "Back o'Skidda". There is a fine circular walk which takes in a handful of the Longlands Fells, crowned by Great Sca Fell and including the amusingly-named Great Cockup.

Distance: 8 miles/13km	*fellwalking although care*
Height gain:	*is needed with*
2,000ft/600m	*navigation in mist.*
Walking time: 5 hours	***Start/Finish:*** *Longlands.*
Type of walk: *Simple*	*GR266358.*

Car parking on the minor road between Orthwaite and Longlands is limited. There is a better chance of securing a space beside the bridge at Longlands than on any other stretch of the road, so the route description starts at that point.

Cross the bridge, then use a gate and stile immediately on the right to access a fine green road. Follow this road uphill from Longlands and branch away from a narrow strip of forest trees. The green road rises gently, then begins to fall gently towards a beck called Charleton Gill.

Don't cross Charleton Gill, but start climbing uphill

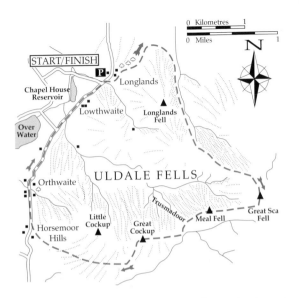

to the right. There is a vague path on the broad moorland slopes of Longlands Fell, but it needs to be looked for carefully at first. Once it is located, it leads in a fairly clear line across the slopes of Longlands Fell. It is like a grassy groove in places, running roughly parallel to Charleton Gill.

Views from within the little dale are restricted, but by turning round there is a splendid view into southern Scotland. Some walkers may wish instead to climb Longlands Fell and claim its summit at 1,580ft/482m. There aren't any obstructions on the ascent and a wider view is gained at an earlier stage. The path in the dale eventually bears left and continues towards Great Sca Fell. It remains clear throughout the ascent, picking its way up a broad and grassy slope. It does not cross the highest point on Great Sca Fell, and this needs to be borne in mind in mist. There is a path heading off to the right which visits both of Great Sca Fell's cairned summits, the highest one standing at 2,131ft/651m.

Views from the top of Great Sca Fell take in precious little of the Lake District. The nearby fells are unremarkable moorland swellings, while other fells are rather distant. Looking northwards and westwards towards Scotland and the Solway Firth, however, the scene is altogether more extensive and interesting. Hills are ranged from Galloway to the Cheviots, with the North Pennines and Isle of Man also featuring in clear conditions.

There is no view of Meal Fell to the west, and no path leading towards it either, but this is the direction to take when leaving Great Sca Fell. Meal Fell comes into view as the slope of Great Sca Fell runs down gently to a gap. A short climb from the gap leads to the summit and a handful of small cairns. There is a bit of outcropping rock and a tumbled cairn shelter.

Continue more south-westwards to descend to the next gap, which is the narrow cleft of Trusmadoor. Looking across the gap, a steep face of slaty scree can be seen, and it is best to avoid this by keeping well to the left. A narrow path will be found running up along a minor rocky edge sprouting bilberry and heather. Simply aim straight for the summit of Great Cockup at 1,725ft/526m.

As the walk is gradually progressing out of the fells, the scene across the Solway opens up even more, while lofty Skiddaw is seen to good effect.

To descend, first continue along the crest of the fell to reach a stone shooting butt on a shoulder, then veer to the left and descend on a heathery slope. Aim for a green fold in the fellside and turn right there to pick up and follow a path. This leads down to a farm access track, where another right turn leads to a gate and a minor road. Turn right yet again to pass through the little hamlet of Orthwaite. Note the lovely Orthwaite Hall in passing. The minor road enjoys a view across Over Water as it runs downhill, then it climbs over a brow at Lowthwaite and overlooks Chapel House Reservoir. A short descent leads back to the parking space at the bridge near Longlands.

5 Fell Side and High Pike

The last Lakeland fell before the plains of Carlisle is the huge moorland swelling of High Pike. Its broad slopes have been pitted and scarred by miners, but its gentle lines still dominate the countryside around Caldbeck as they have done for centuries. The mines are all quiet now, long abandoned and visited only by students of geology. Walkers will find a high degree of solitude in the area, although the Cumbria Way crosses High Pike and the fell is being visited more and more often.

Distance: 7 miles/11km	fellwalking with some care needed on top in mist.
Height gain: 1,575ft/480m	**Start/Finish:** Fell Side, near Caldbeck.
Walking time: 4 hours	GR304374.
Type of walk: Simple	

Fell Side is a tiny village on a loop of minor road near Caldbeck. Its only facilities are the Fellside Centre and a telephone box. There is space to park a few cars near Fellside Farm, so that makes a convenient starting point for a walk taking in Roughton Gill and High Pike.

Follow the track uphill from the parking space near Fellside Farm. Pass through a gate at the end of the track and turn right to follow another track. There is a prominent rock which has been painted to indicate the way to Roughton Gill and the

Caldbeck Fells. The track crosses a number of small gills either using fords or footbridges. It runs parallel to the course of Dale Beck on the way to the horrendously scarred dale head. Heaps of spoil and ruined buildings abound around the old mining site at Roughton Gill.

Looking at the scene of devastation, explorers might be tempted to climb up into a rocky gill where there are waterfalls and a few trees. The route, however, heads off to the left and climbs up around the craggy fellside before being drawn into a narrow valley. There is only a sparse path, so feel free to pick any reasonable route up and around the fellside. There is a small beck in the valley at first, but as height is gained the walk continues on the dry bed of the valley with scree slopes to the right. Emerging from the top of the valley there is a broad moorland gap to cross where a few boulders lie scattered around.

Look ahead while walking across the moorland to spot a small wooden hut on Great Lingy Hill. This hut is kept in reasonable condition and is left open for the use of passing walkers. A notice requests that it is left in good order, as around a thousand walkers use it each year. Some stay overnight by design, while others use it more as an emergency shelter when they are caught out in foul weather. There may be a "bothy book" listing recent visitors.

From the hut, follow a clear path towards High Pike. There is a slight moorland rise to cross before the slopes of High Pike lead to the summit at 2,157ft/658m. This is an unmistakeable point as

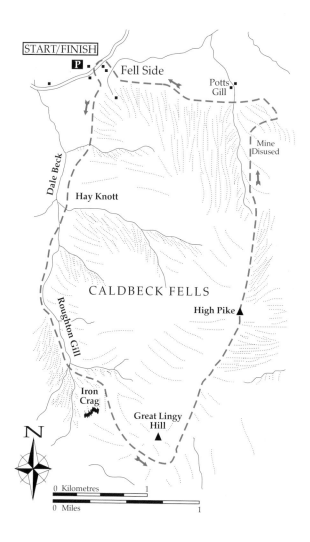

START/FINISH

Fell Side

Potts Gill

Mine Disused

Dale Beck

Hay Knott

CALDBECK FELLS

Roughton Gill

High Pike ▲

Iron Crag

Great Lingy Hill ▲

N

0 Kilometres 1

0 Miles 1

there is so much distinctive summit furniture. There is a trig point, a large cairn, and a stone memorial seat for anyone who wishes to rest in comfort. Formerly, the memorial seat was wrought iron, but it was replaced with a stone seat after several sheep got their horns caught in the metalwork!

The remote aloofness of High Pike makes it a fine viewpoint. Northwards is a great stretch of low country before ranks of hills raise their profiles in southern Scotland. Looking southwards, the country "Back o'Skidda" naturally features the summits of Skiddaw and Blencathra, while more distantly parts of the Scafell and High Street ranges can be distinguished. The North Pennines may also feature prominently in clear weather.

Walk roughly northwards to leave the summit of High Pike. The broad moorland slopes are largely pathless, and the only thing to keep an eye open for are the holes of former mines. In mist it would be a good idea to take a compass bearing for the long descent. Eventually, other paths come into view, and the one to follow continues roughly northwards downhill. There is a sweeping zigzag on a track above the secluded farmstead of Potts Gill. Don't be drawn on to the lower fields, but turn left and follow a path parallel to the boundary wall on the fellside above Potts Gill. The path climbs gently uphill and passes the next farm at Little Fellside, then finally runs back towards Fell Side, where the walk started.

6 Carrock Fell

An old saying relates that "Caldbeck Fells are worth all England else" and in terms of its rich mineral wealth this may well be true. Carrock Fell is unusual in Lakeland because it is composed of a rock known as gabbro. More unusually, this rock lies in contact with a granitic mass, which is in many respects like two opposites coming into contact. The resultant strange mix of minerals includes some which are not found elsewhere in the country, and so Carrock Fell has immense interest for geologists. It also offers a good fellwalk.

Distance:
6 miles/10km
Height gain:
1,575ft/480m
Walking time: 4 hours
Type of walk: Mostly
easy fellwalking although the descent is steep and rugged.
Start/Finish: Carrock Beck, near High Row. GR350351.

Motorists taking the fellside road from Mosedale to Hesket Newmarket find themselves crossing the open lower slopes of Carrock Fell, then they have to ford Carrock Beck. There are parking spaces beside the road on the pull uphill from the beck. Alternatively, any walkers using the splendid Carrock Fell Youth Hostel at High Row can walk across a boggy slope often ablaze with yellow gorse to reach the start of this walk.

A track runs off the minor road on to Caldbeck Common, and there is a small sign bearing the name of the common. Follow the track for a short way, then head off to the right and pick up the course of a grassy track which runs up a slope of bracken. Keep heading up this slope, looking forwards to gauge the way through a criss-crossing network of paths. As a general rule, always choose the path which makes the most direct progress uphill. As height is gained, it is a good idea to move slightly to the left so that there are opportunities to look down into the valley drained by Carrock Beck.

A band of mining spoil is reached on the slopes of High Pike, and at this point turn left to follow a rather gritty track which cuts across the upper flank of the hill. If the day is clear, it is worth climbing to the top of High Pike, reaching the summit trig point, cairn and stone seat at 2,157ft/658m.

The views prove really extensive, stretching to embrace southern Scotland, the North Pennines and all the fells "Back o'Skidda". If a summit bid is not made, then follow the gritty mining track onwards around the head of the valley.

Look out for a vague path cutting off to the right, not down into the valley, but out towards the crest of Miton Hill. There is a rather better trodden path over Miton Hill which passes a couple of cairns on the broad moorland crest. As progress is made further along the crest the ground becomes rockier and the rugged upper slopes of Carrock Fell are reached.

On the final ascent, look out for traces of a rough wall of

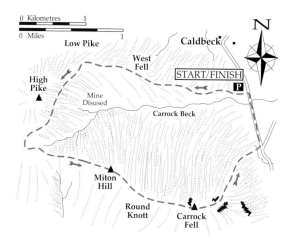

masonry which encloses the summit area. This is the boundary wall of a Bronze Age hill fort, where residents would have had a fine view across the surrounding countryside. The summit cairn stands at 2,174ft/662m just inside the enclosure of the hill fort.

The descent is roughly north-eastwards, from the summit of Carrock Fell towards a road junction far below. Don't walk straight downhill in this direction, but make use of a series of vague paths which have been trodden on the bouldery, bilberry covered slopes. Straying too far to the right brings more and more rocky ground underfoot, while keeping to the left gives a better chance of seeing a clear run-out on to the lower slopes of bracken later.

Pick a way down towards the road junction, then turn left to follow the road across the common.

There is a slight rise before the ford through Carrock Beck is reached. There is no need to splash through like the cars must, as there is a footbridge alongside.

BLENCATHRA

Blencathra displays a most arresting mountain profile when seen from the south. Its northern slopes are mostly moorland, but there is an exception where the knife-edge ridge of Sharp Edge protrudes from the fell. The sprawling slopes of Blencathra spread in all directions and link with nearby fells, so that there is plenty of scope for varied routes.

Of the three routes described in this section, the first one is around Souter Fell, Bowscale Fell and Bannerdale. It doesn't set foot on Blencathra, but it does allow a view of its lesser-seen northern slopes, as well as a chance to study Sharp Edge without getting to grips with it. In any case, the fells near to Blencathra are always quieter than their taller neighbour and are well worth exploring.

When the time comes to tackle Blencathra, there are two remarkably different routes which can be considered. Adventurous walkers who have a good head for heights and are agile enough to get to grips with the rock can enjoy an entertaining traverse of Sharp Edge and the Hall's Fell Ridge. Those who prefer to proceed more cautiously can enjoy a route which traverses along the high crest of Blencathra, offering views of its rugged ridges and ravines, without the need to grapple with them.

There is a bus service between Penrith and Keswick which passes Blencathra, and it is possible to cover all three walks using that service, although the walk taking in Bannerdale would need to be restructured to start from Scales. There is only a handful of villages around Blencathra and all offer at least an inn where refreshments can be obtained.

Blencathra has the rather unfortunate nickname of "Saddleback", which refers to the shape of its summit crest when seen from certain viewpoints. Blencathra is a fine name for a fine fell. It is a name of some antiquity and should be preserved.

Another echo from the past concerns a strange happening on Souther Fell. In 1745 an army was observed marching along its crest, but on closer inspection there was no trace of it, and no sign of it anywhere else in the area. The walk described over Souther Fell tells you more.

7 Souther Fell and Bannerdale

This walk around Souther Fell, Bowscale Fell and Bannerdale should be fairly quiet, although there may well be several walkers observed marching towards Sharp Edge on Blencathra. In 1745 an entire army was observed to march across the crest of Souther Fell, including men, horses and waggons. They appeared at one end of the crest and disappeared at the other, and no-one saw them in any other part of the area. On closer inspection, not a blade of grass on the fell had been disturbed and the sighting remains a mystery.

Distance: 7 miles/11km	*fellwalking with careful route finding needed on top in mist.*
Height gain: 2,000ft/610m	**Start/Finish:** Mungrisdale.
Walking time: 4 hours	GR362303.
Type of walk: Moderate	

Parking is fairly limited around the tiny village of Mungrisdale. Patrons of the Mill Inn may be able to arrange to park there, otherwise use the space beside a telephone box in the village and don't forget to leave an offering in the nearby honesty box.

Walk out of Mungrisdale via the Mill Inn and follow a minor road until a gateway leads out on to the open fell. There is a rise on the road, and

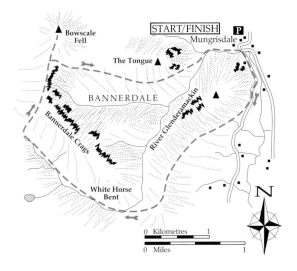

around that point look out for a rutted path leading up into the bracken.

The path is not marked on OS maps, but it is marked on Harvey's maps and it becomes clearer as height is gained. Follow it diagonally across the slopes of Souther Fell, and when it becomes vague towards the top of the fell, continue its line to gain the summit crest. The true summit of the fell stands at 1,680ft/522m, but it isn't crossed on this walk. Instead, follow the crest of the fell onwards to descend to the gap above Mousthwaite Comb.

A path heads off to the right from the gap and descends further to cross a wooden bridge over the River Glenderamackin. Turn left after crossing the river and follow a path running upstream. On the opposite side of the river there may be several other walkers heading for Sharp Edge and Blencathra. Looking ahead towards Sharp Edge, some of them may already be distinguished, gingerly picking their way along the rocky edge. Continue walking upstream to reach a grassy gap at the head of the valley.

There are a number of paths leading away from the grassy gap. There is one which turns to the extreme right, but don't follow it. Instead, take the next one off to the right and follow it up a grassy slope. The path leads across a broad and boggy moorland, then runs straight to the summit of Bowscale Fell. A cairn shelter stands on the summit at 2,300ft/702m. As this is the highest point gained on the walk, it is worth spending time studying the extensive view.

While Blencathra looms large to the south, the Helvellyn and High Street fells can be seen to one side, as well as the North Pennines more distantly. To the other side of Blencathra, the view takes in fells around Buttermere. The fine rolling hills "Back o'Skidda" are well displayed and northwards there are views into southern Scotland.

Retrace steps from the summit of Bowscale Fell, down to a point where a small cairn on a broad and boggy gap marks an intersection of paths. Turn left at this point and follow a path towards Bannerdale Crags. The path joins another path which picks a way along the rim of Bannerdale Crags. Follow the most obvious route onwards, down into Bannerdale. The path crosses slopes of bracken and is perfectly clear throughout the descent. It turns around the blunt end of The Tongue, crosses a bridge over Bullfell Beck and runs straight back to the little village of Mungrisdale. The Mill Inn offers food and drink.

Walkers who are relying on bus services may find Mungrisdale an inconvenient place to start this walk. The route is easily restructured using Scales as a starting point on the Penrith to Keswick bus service. The walk, in this instance, would start and finish using the path through Mousthwaite Comb.

8 Blencathra via Sharp Edge

Sooner or later those who walk in the Lake District begin to hear about Sharp Edge on Blencathra. Tales of its ascent vary considerably, depending on how people's experiences of scrambling on rock vary. There are many walkers who would have no problem at all on Sharp Edge in clear, dry weather. There are others who simply don't have the necessary head for heights, or simply lack confidence in exposed locations. In this route, Sharp Edge is coupled with the Hall's Fell Ridge on Blencathra.

Distance: 6 miles/10km	Strenuous fellwalking with some rocky stretches requiring scrambling skills.
Height gain: 2,400ft/730m	
Walking time: 4 hours	**Start/Finish:** Threlkeld.
Type of walk:	GR323254.

Blencathra is a wonderfully romantic name, and yet many walkers refer to it as "Saddleback". This is unfortunate, and in any case the "saddle" is apparent only in certain views. Despite throwing out shoulders in most directions, there is only one sizable village on the flanks of Blencathra, and that is Threlkeld. It has an inn with a parking space opposite and makes a fine place to start and finish the walk. An alternative starting point would be at another inn at nearby Scales.

Park opposite the Horse and Farrier Inn at Threlkeld and walk towards the main road, as if heading for Penrith. Before reaching the main road, however, turn left up a minor road to pass the farm at Gategill. Baying foxhounds will confirm that the correct course has been taken. Walk above the farm, then turn right to start traversing across the lower slopes of Blencathra.

Streams running down from three astoundingly chaotic stony ravines are crossed. Gate Gill is crossed first, then Doddick Gill and finally Scaley Beck. A path begins climbing above Scales, where an inn can be seen in the tiny hamlet. The path steepens as it enters the hollow of Mousthwaite Comb and eventually runs close to a grassy gap. Turn left around the slope of the fell – not climbing straight uphill, but more contouring around the slope to enter the valley of the River Glenderamackin.

The path stays well above the River Glenderamackin and runs upstream. Look out for another path heading off to the left later, which climbs up to Scales Tarn. The tarn is overshadowed by dark crags, from which projects the serrated knife-edge ridge of Sharp Edge. There may already be other people in view carefully picking their way along the rocky crest.

All that is needed on Sharp Edge is a head for heights, a steady pair of feet and the willingness to use hands for balance from time to time. There is no rock climbing involved, although the edge is bounded by very steep rock faces. Dry weather is essential, as rain or even a damp

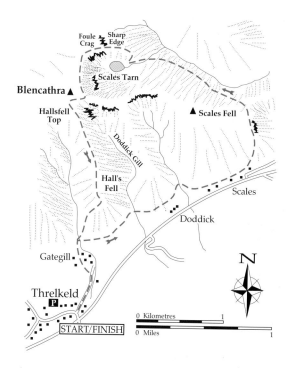

Foule Crag
Sharp Edge
Scales Tarn
Blencathra ▲
Hallsfell Top
Doddick Gill
▲ Scales Fell
Hall's Fell
Scales
Doddick
Gategill
Threlkeld
P
START/FINISH
N
0 Kilometres 1
0 Miles 1

*mist can make the rock treacherously slippery underfoot.
Snow and ice cover rule out any chance of an ordinary
walker traversing the edge.*

Walk along the well blazed stony path towards
Sharp Edge. By degrees, there is more and more
rock, but the path continues to be clear all the way
along the rugged crest. Gradually, the bounding
slopes steepen, and sometimes it is necessary to
proceed along a very narrow edge. Keep to those
routes which show that others have passed

frequently that way before. Trying to descend or otherwise outflank rocky stretches often leads into difficulty. There is no dishonour in crawling for short stretches, but when the path allows, stand tall and walk! The rocky edge becomes less clearly defined later, and the final part of the ascent involves clawing a way up a messy slope to reach the top of Foule Crag. Beyond that is a simple dome of grass.

From the top of Foule Crag to the summit of Blencathra, the walk is across the broad, grassy saddle which gives rise to Blencathra's lamentable alternative name. A feature of note on the saddle is a prominent cross composed of quartz-streaked stones gathered from the fell. Walkers have been adding to this for decades, so that it grows larger all the time. It has gained a twin nearby. The summit of Blencathra stands at 2,847ft/868m. There is no trig point, no towering cairn, nothing to proclaim this lordly height except a small heap of slaty stones. The view down the front of Blencathra displays awesome stony slopes and rocky ridges. Looking around the "Back o'Skidda" reveals a host of rolling hills and bleak moorlands. Most of the prominent Lakeland summits are in view, including the High Street, Helvellyn, Coniston, Langdale, Scafell, Buttermere and Newlands fells. The North Pennines and southern Scotland feature more distantly in clear weather.

The descent is literally straight forward. Step down from the summit of Blencathra on to the rugged Hall's Fell Ridge. There is a well trodden path, though it is best to take this slowly and steadily as there are some very steep slopes along the way. It is hardly the sort of scrambling experienced on

Sharp Edge, but there are a couple of little rock-steps which need to be passed with care on the way down.

Take care to bear to the right on the way down Hall's Fell, so that a path is followed which leads back over the stream of Gate Gill. A left turn after crossing leads back past Gategill Farm and its howling hounds. Simply retrace steps along the road to return to Threlkeld.

9 Blencathra

When seen from the south, the sprawling fell of Blencathra has an excellent symmetry. Its front face is riven with deep ravines separated by rocky ridges, while Scales Fell and Blease Fell form rounded buttresses to the east and west. It looks good and indeed it is good. The following walk explores the whole face of Blencathra, from its lower slopes around Threlkeld and Scales, all the way along its summit crest, offering views along its many ridges and into its awesome ravines. Generally, easy paths are used throughout.

Distance: 8 miles/13km	straightforward walking,
Height gain:	although care is needed
2,360ft/720m	in mist.
Walking time: 4 hours	**Start/Finish:** Threlkeld.
Type of walk: Fairly	GR323254.

Park at the space opposite the Horse and Farrier in Threlkeld and walk towards the main road, as if leaving the village for Penrith. Before reaching the main road, turn left up a minor road to pass the fellside farm at Gategill. Walk above the farm, then turn right to start following a path across the lower slopes of Blencathra. Streams are crossed which run down from three immensely rugged ravines. Gate Gill is crossed first, then Doddick Gill, followed by Scaley Beck.

A path climbs above Scales, which is no more than

a tiny hamlet with an inn. The path steepens as it enters the brackeny hollow of Mousthwaite Comb. As this path is followed uphill, a rocky edge is reached and if an eye is kept on the ground a path should be spotted heading off to the left. This path zigzags uphill on the bracken and grass slopes of Scales Fell. If located, it makes a good start to the ascent. If for any reason it is not located, then head uphill anyway and hope to link with its course at a higher level. Avoid any paths which lead into the valley of the River Glenderamackin.

Some walkers may find the slope tedious, but it is without any real difficulty apart from navigation in mist. There is no need to scramble on rocky ground as on many other ascents. As the path rises it runs along a rugged edge overlooking Scaley Beck. It continues along and passes the top of the Doddick Fell ridge. On the final ascent to the summit of Blencathra, the eye is drawn into the rugged ravine of Doddick Gill. The top of Blencathra rises to 2,847ft/868m and bears no more than a small heap of slaty stones.

Views are exceptionally wide ranging, embracing the empty country "Back o'Skidda", the distant North Pennines, the High Street and Helvellyn ranges, the Coniston, Langdale and Scafell groups, along with the Buttermere and Newlands fells. Northwards there may be ranks of hills in southern Scotland. Close to hand is Hall's Fell Ridge, falling away steeply underfoot.

Continuing the walk, simply stick to the top of the edge overlooking the dramatic southern face of Blencathra. The ground underfoot is always safe

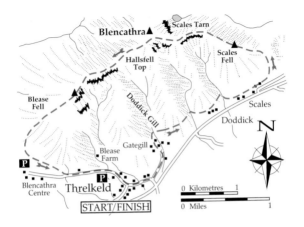

and easy, despite the steep and rocky terrain falling away to the left. There are ample opportunities to stand and stare into the depths on the way to Blease Fell. The vast hollow drained by Gate Gill is seen first, and the walk leads on past the ridge falling to Gategill Fell. Blease Gill trickles down through the next great hollow, before the minor hump of Blease Fell is gained. This is a fine stance from which to observe the slopes of Skiddaw.

Take care over the descent, especially in misty conditions, as paths on the broad fellside can be vague in places. It is possible to descend a direct and very steep slope towards Blease Farm, but it is kinder on the knees to walk roughly south-westwards towards the Blease Inn Centre. There is a path of sorts which needs to be looked for carefully in places. It finally describes a broad, sweeping zigzag before landing on a minor road beside the Centre.

All that remains is to turn left and follow the minor road back to Threlkeld. The open fellside is left behind and the road passes High Row Farm on the way back into the village.

ST. JOHN'S IN THE VALE

To many travellers, St. John's in the Vale is no more than a short cut from one main road to another. It's worth stopping sometime and enjoying this lovely valley for its own sake. It is bounded by fearsome rock walls in places, but there are lines of access to the higher fells. St. John's in the Vale Church is not immediately apparent to casual visitors, but it can

be found sitting on a gap between High Rigg and Low Rigg. There is a youth centre attached which introduces many youngsters to the outdoors. Another feature of note is the sky above Clough Head. This is sometimes filled with the most amazing assortment of

St John's in the Vale church

hang-gliders and parapentes in all shapes and colours. The thermals are often perfect for taking to the air. Sometimes one of the participants will break from the pack and soar effortlessly across The Dodds above St. John's in the Vale.

Two walks are offered from St. John's in the Vale. There is an easy walk over High Rigg, which turns out to be very hummocky and seems more extensive than the map leads walkers to believe. A gentler return along the foot of the fell can be extended to take in neighbouring Low Rigg as well.

Christine Isherwood

The other walk climbs up what looks like an impossibly steep and rocky fellside, then enjoys a gentler romp over the rounded, grassy hills of The Dodds. Strong fellwalkers might prefer to use The Dodds as giant stepping stones towards Helvellyn, which looks tantalisingly close from Stybarrow Dodd. As most of the ascent has already been achieved, the remaining climbing towards Helvellyn is of little consequence.

Facilities in St. John's in the Vale are extremely limited. There is a simple Youth Hostel at Legburthwaite, farmhouse B&B accommodation and the chance to obtain teas and snacks. The nearest pub is the King's Head Hotel at Thirlspot, although Keswick isn't far away by road. There are regular bus services at either end of the vale, but no buses pass along the road through the vale.

This book covers walks in the eastern half of the Lake District. There is a companion volume covering walks in the western half, offering other routes near St. John's in the Vale, such as a circuit around Thirlmere and a walk over the fells to Watendlath.

10 High Rigg

Some little fells are not at all abashed by their lack of height. Some prove to be extremely rugged and are like a whole range of fells in their own right. High Rigg is such a fell. It is surrounded by much higher fells, including Skiddaw, Blencathra, Clough Head and Bleaberry Fell, and yet it presents a rugged switchback of tops and is flanked by some particularly rocky slopes. It stands jammed in the throat of St. John's in the Vale, offering a fine little fellwalk with good views of its loftier neighbours.

Distance: 7 miles/11km	*a moderate fellwalk*
Height gain:	*along a knobbly ridge.*
1,375ft/420m	**Start/Finish:**
Walking time: 4 hours	*Smaithwaite Bridge,*
Type of walk: An easy	*Legburthwaite.*
walk at first followed by	*GR315195.*

There is a regular bus service passing Legburthwaite between Keswick and Grasmere. Cars can also be parked near Legburthwaite and the walk can be started at Smaithwaite Bridge.

The walk first traverses around the foot of High Rigg and Low Rigg before tracing a switchback route over the tops. A good path leads through oakwoods and runs parallel to the course of St. John's Beck as it leaves Smaithwaite Bridge. The path follows a high bank, then reaches Low Bridge

End Farm, where teas and snacks may be offered. The farmhouse is reputed to be haunted by a number of ghosts!

Leave Low Bridge End Farm and continue along the foot of the fell, passing a variety of trees. The path later climbs slightly and becomes a clear track bounded by grass, featuring less trees. Blencathra fills the northward prospect, while Clough Head raises fearsome crags and gullies across the vale. When the track reaches a road, there is a decision to be made. A short walk can be enjoyed by turning left for the Diocesan Youth Centre, but a longer walk can be savoured by turning right to make a circuit over Low Rigg first.

Turn right and follow the road downhill. Go through a gate, then turn left along a farm access track. Beyond the farmhouse a gate is marked with a sign for the footpath. Follow the field path straight onwards and look out for steps on the left which lead up into the next field. The exit from this field is by a gate near some caravans. When a minor road is joined, turn left to follow it uphill only a short way. There is a signpost reading "St. John's in the Vale Church via Tewet Tarn" at the point where walkers leave the road.

Walk uphill from the road and follow waymark posts and arrows. These indicate the way through fields and reveal the stiles in walls or fences which need to be crossed. Climb almost to the summit of Low Rigg, then drift gradually downhill towards the little church and the Diocesan Youth Centre. Motorists sometimes drive to this point and make a

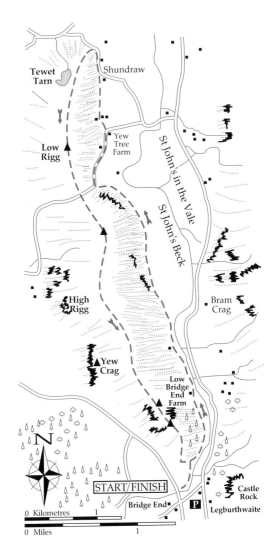

Tewet
Tarn

Shundraw

Low
Rigg

Yew
Tree Farm

St John's in the Vale

St John's Beck

High
Rigg

Bram
Crag

Yew
Crag

Low
Bridge
End
Farm

N

START/FINISH

Castle
Rock

Bridge End

P

Legburthwaite

0 Kilometres 1

0 Miles 1

short ascent to the summit of High Rigg, which is the next objective on the walk.

Climb straight uphill from the Youth Centre, going through a little gate before following a grassy path further uphill. The summit of High Rigg is soon gained and it bears a cairn at 1,163ft/355m.

Although only a lowly height, High Rigg is the highest point reached on this walk, and the only point from which the whole of the surroundings can be appreciated at once. Clough Head and Blencathra continue to dominate the scene, with Skiddaw also well displayed. Surprisingly, there are views of the Buttermere Fells. The boggy dome of Ullscarf and the flanks of the Helvellyn range are ranked either side of Thirlmere.

Follow the path away from the summit, along the hummocky crest of the fell. There is plenty of rock and bracken, and the fell is divided by a number of drystone walls. Cross a stile over a wall to continue further along the rugged crest. Even with a careful study of the map, it is often difficult to gauge exactly what position has been reached. Cross a stile over a fence, then stay on the path to reach a rocky little gap in the crest. The path begins to descend a rough and steep slope where there are attractive stands of pine trees. At a lower level oaks are dominant, and a right turn leads back on to the main road near Smaithwaite Bridge.

11 The Dodds

The Dodds are situated at the northernmost end of the Helvellyn range and have something of a Jekyll and Hyde character. The summits of these fells are uniformly rolling and grassy, but the flanks falling into St. John's in the Vale are often exceptionally rocky and in many places completely out of bounds to mere walkers. There are ways up and down The Dodds, while the walk along the summit crest is easily accomplished in fine weather. Note that the arrangment of the tops is complicated and navigational skills are required in mist.

Distance:
9 miles/14.5km
Height gain:
2,870ft/875m
Walking time: 6 hours
Type of walk: A steep
and strenuous climb
followed by easier
fellwalking.
Start/Finish:
Legburthwaite.
GR318190.

Legburthwaite has a small amount of parking available and is also on a good bus service running between Grasmere and Keswick.

Start the walk by following the B5322 road through St. John's in the Vale. At the start, the Castle Rock of Triermain stands high above the road, and there are other steep and rocky slopes on both sides of the road. There is also an access road on the left leading to farmhouse teas at Low Bridge End Farm, if these are required. Enjoy the scenery as the road walk progresses, but look out for the private access road on the right which leads into Bram Crag Quarry. Don't follow this road, but a little further along, also on the right, a series of stiles give access to the open fell above the site of the quarry.

It looks as if there is no way forward, but this ascent uses an old path known as Fisher's Wife's Rake. Look carefully for it and take the ascent slowly and steadily. By carefully casting an eye across the steep scree slopes, it is possible to discern the faint traces of a zigzag path. Even if this is not spotted, head up the scree. The scree seems to spill from a rather ferocious looking gully, and although walkers are drawn towards the gully, it is not recommended to follow it all the way. Instead, look very carefully to the right and a path will be seen leaving the scree slope and picking its way around a steep and rocky slope. This part of Fisher's Wife's Rake is much easier to follow and it zigzags up the rugged slope to emerge on the open fell above. The path leads to a sheepfold known as Jim's Fold. Continue more gently uphill aiming roughly north-east to reach the top of Clough Head.

The summit of Clough Head bears a cairn and a trig point at 2,381ft/726m. There is a great sense of depth to the northward view, which faces Blencathra's most dramatic slopes. Neighbouring Skiddaw and all its accompanying fells also feature well. Part of the High Street and Helvellyn ranges are in view, but a much greater spread of fells is arranged from south to west, including the Coniston, Langdale, Scafell, Buttermere and Newlands groups. Again, these fells are seen across the gulf containing Thirlmere, giving a good depth to the view. If the weather is misty, not only will there be no view, but the whole walk needs to be covered on compass bearings as the main crest of The Dodds zigzags wildly.

Heading southwards from Clough Head a gentle path crosses a broad and sometimes boggy gap and reaches the prominent rocky outcrop of Calfhow Pike. A pronounced change of direction is needed as the path swings gradually eastwards on the long, grassy slope leading up on to Great Dodd. The summit stands at 2,807ft/858m and offers an extensive view. Walkers who are flagging, however, may have spotted paths bypassing the summit and heading more directly for Watson's Dodd.

From the top of Great Dodd, another sudden change of direction is needed to reach Watson's Dodd. The line of descent is roughly south-west. There are walkers who feel drawn all the way on to the top of Watson's Dodd, but it is no more than a broad swelling on the grassy crest of The Dodds, and other walkers will be content to follow a clear path which omits it from the itinerary. Whatever line is chosen, the path again courses through the compass points and begins to drift almost south-east towards Stybarrow Dodd.

The top of Stybarrow Dodd is graced by twin summits separated by a shallow grassy saddle. The highest point is reached first at 2,770ft/846m, and in mist it is important to note that the rival summit is south-west of that point. Leaving Stybarrow Dodd, the last of The Dodds on this walk, follow a path running southwards to the top of the Sticks Pass.

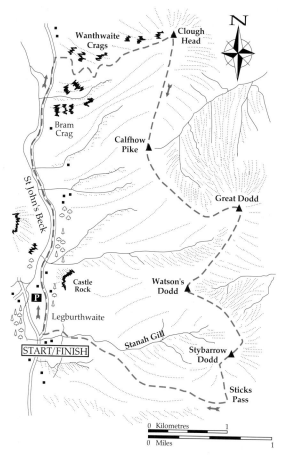

In clear weather, the whole of the Helvellyn range beckons, and walkers who have struggled up on to Clough Head may feel that an extension is in order. By

all means head in that direction, but for the time being this walk is drawing to a conclusion.

Turn right to start following Sticks Pass downhill. The line of the path is reasonably distinct throughout the descent. The grassy slopes begin to steepen and a sheepfold is reached, which is perched overlooking Stanah Gill. The lower slopes are covered in bracken and are more rugged. As Legburthwaite is reached, note how water is drawn off along an artificial channel to feed the nearby reservoir of Thirlmere.

WYTHBURN

In a sense, Wythburn is no more. The little hamlet consisted of a church, an inn and a handful of other buildings. With the construction of the reservoir of Thirlmere in the 1890s, the nearby meadows were submerged and the few buildings making up Wythburn were demolished. Only the church was spared, and even this has been obscured from view by the planting of ranks of conifers around Thirlmere. Lest its name perish from memory, Wythburn is used as the heading for this section.

There are two routes under this heading. One starts from The Swirls and passes Wythburn later, while the other starts and finishes on Dunmail Raise, which is above Wythburn. The route from The Swirls uses a popular path to climb Helvellyn, then uses a zigzagging pony track to descend towards Wythburn. This is one of the easiest ways to cross Helvellyn, but it offers few chances to see the rugged crags and ridges which lie on the other side of the fell. It is included primarily for those who do not wish to grapple with Striding Edge and Swirral Edge, which are described elsewhere in this guide.

The walk from the top of Dunmail Raise takes in the solitary fell of Seat Sandal. This could stake a claim to being the centre of the Lake District if only because water falling on to its slopes reaches the sea at three remarkably distant points.

Both the walks are easily accessed using regular bus services between Ambleside, Grasmere and Keswick. If using the buses, be sure to give the driver plenty of notice as it is not always easy to stop at some points along the road. Car parks used on these walks are small and can become crowded in the peak season. Other facilities are few, limited to a couple of roadside inns off the course of both the walks. However, Keswick and Grasmere are easily reached by car or bus after the walks and they both offer a full range of services, including abundant accommodation, shops, pubs and restaurants.

This book covers walks in the eastern half of the Lake District. There is another volume offering walks in the western half. Wythburn and Thirlmere are on the dividing line, so the companion guide gives routes around Thirlmere, over the fells to Watendlath, around Grasmere and Helm Crag, and further westwards to the coast at Ravenglass.

12 Helvellyn and Wythburn

There are all sorts of ways to bring Helvellyn underfoot. The classic tour around Striding Edge and Swirral Edge is described in another part of this book. The route offered here uses easier paths. Note the word "easier" and not "easy" as this is one of the highest mountains in the Lake District and it requires some effort to make a summit bid. The circuit described uses a fairly direct ascent from Thirlspot coupled with a slightly more gently graded descent to Wythburn.

Distance: 7 miles/11km **Height gain:** 2,790ft/850m **Walking time:** 4 hours **Type of walk:** Strenuous	fellwalking in places, but not recommended in poor visibility. **Start/Finish:** The Swirls car park, near Thirlspot. GR317168.

The Swirls car park lies in between the King's Head Hotel at Thirlspot and the forested shores of Thirlmere. There is a toilet block beside the car park and a number of paths lead away into the countryside.

The path to follow is the one climbing uphill alongside the forest, which later breaks away from the top side of the forest and follows the course of Helvellyn Gill upstream. The path is steep practically from the start and gets steeper later, so it is advisable to take the climbing slowly and steadily.

There has been some backbreaking reconstruction work done on this line of ascent, particularly on the screes around Browncove Crags. It is important that walkers stick to the reconstructed path and do not cause unsightly erosion and damage by scrambling across the shifting screes. The path zigzags up the slope to take some of the effort out of the gradient and has a firm surface throughout.

At the top of the steep and rocky ascent, the path becomes much gentler and proceeds just short of the summit of Helvellyn Lower Man. Most walkers seem intent on reaching the top of Helvellyn and so have no time for minor summits along the way. There is a trig point perched on Helvellyn's steep edge overlooking Red Tarn. It stands at an altitude of 3,118ft/950m, although the area is relatively broad and flat.

Take in the extensive views, which in crystal clear weather can stretch from The Cheviots to the mountains of Snowdonia. More likely the distant views will be marked by the long line of the Pennines and closer to hand every notable group of Lakeland fells will be seen. It is a panorama to savour and keen fellwalkers will be able to call out the name of virtually every hump and bump in view.

In nasty weather there is no point in lingering on the summit, though it is wise to note the existence of a cross-shelter a short distance to the south-west. This is often so crowded with walkers at lunchtime that it resembles a

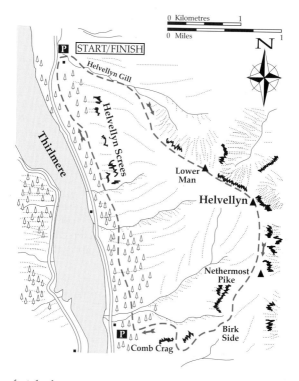

P START/FINISH

Helvellyn Gill

Helvellyn Screes

Thirlmere

Lower Man

Helvellyn

Nethermost Pike

P

Comb Crag

Birk Side

fast food restaurant! By passing the shelter, walkers are already on the path leading away from the summit. Keep to the most well-blazed route, a gritty pedestrian highway running roughly southwards.

At a fork in the track, where it is necessary to keep to the right to continue the descent, the route drops easily down the broad slopes of Nethermost Pike, then later begins to steepen and cross rougher ground. There are all sorts of zigzags and changes of direction on the descent, but the path remains clear throughout and cuts through Comb Crags to reach the top edge of a forest.

Continue the descent through the forest, to reach the main road, if you can time your descent to coincide with one of the regular buses passing Wythburn. Otherwise, turn right along a clear path before reaching Wythburn Church. The path contours across the forested slope and is equipped with a footbridge to cross Comb Gill and Whelpside Gill. Continue following the path through the forest, rising occasionally and crossing other streams on the slope. It is hard to gauge progress when the trees obscure the view, but by progressing ever onwards the path eventually rises towards The Swirls, then suddenly descends and emerges at The Swirls car park.

13 Seat Sandal

Those who would like to journey to the centre of the Lake District may wonder just where the centre is supposed to be. Lines can be drawn across the length and breadth of the area and their intersection could be considered the centre. Motorists may regard Dunmail Raise as the centre. In terms of watersheds, the undisputed centre of the Lake District is Seat Sandal. Water falling on it can drain to the Solway Firth via Carlisle, to the Irish Sea via Workington, or southwards to Morecambe Bay. Seat Sandal is the hydrological pivot of the Lake District.

Distance: *5 miles/8km*
Height gain: *1,835ft/560m*
Walking time: *3 hours*
**Type of walk:*

Fellwalking which involves some steep and rugged slopes.
Start/Finish: *Dunmail Raise. GR330111.*

Dunmail Raise has the appearance of frontier country. It was for a long time on the dividing line between Cumberland and Westmorland, and it certainly divides the northern half of Lakeland from the southern half, as well as the east from the west. Cars can be parked on the Grasmere side of the gap, in a parking space close to the Achille Ratti climbing hut.

Start the walk by heading towards the top of the gap. There is no need to walk on the busy road, as there is access to the fellside.

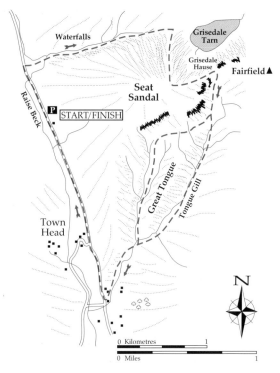

Take note of the cairn which lies stranded in the middle of the dual carriageway. According to an old story it was raised in the year 945 when a Cumberland king by the name of Dunmail was slain in a fierce battle on the spot.

Eastwards of Dunmail Raise, Raise Beck tumbles down from a hanging valley in between Seat Sandal and Dollywaggon Pike. There is a path alongside it which runs straight upstream and allows views of many little waterfalls as height is gained. Towards the top the path is less steep and the headwaters of Raise Beck are unremarkable. A gap in the fells is reached from where there is a view across to Grisedale Tarn.

Turn right on the gap to follow the course of an old boundary wall up the slopes of Seat Sandal. The steep and grassy slope gradually gives way to easier gradients before the top of the fell is reached at 2,415ft/736m, where a cairn stands away from the boundary wall.

Looking around, the view takes in Grisedale, where the water flows towards Ullswater, the River Eden and the Solway Firth. The Vale of Grasmere holds the River Rothay which flows into Windermere, from where the River Leven flows to Morecambe Bay. A portion of Thirlmere is also in view, where any water not piped to distant Manchester must enter the Derwent system and debouch into the sea at Workington.

Quite apart from hydrological features there are views of the surrounding fells. Fairfield and Dollywaggon Pike are nearby and of greater stature, but looking more westwards the view takes in parts of the Coniston, Langdale, Scafell, Buttermere, Newlands and Skiddaw groups.

To leave the summit, continue to trace the course of the old boundary wall. Its course is over easy ground for a short while, to a sudden dramatic steepening where plenty of rock outcrops. Pick a way carefully down this steep and rugged slope to reach Grisedale Hause. Here, a right turn starts the descent towards Grasmere. There is a fork in the path later, where walkers could either keep descending towards Tongue Gill, or switch to the right and descend by way of Little Tongue Gill. The latter descent is usually quieter, though both routes converge near Tonguegill Force before reaching the main road at Mill Bridge.

Walkers who reached Dunmail Raise by bus might like to head into the village of Grasmere and find food and drink before taking the next bus away, but motorists must turn right and follow the main road from Mill Bridge back up on to Dunmail Raise. If their timing was good a Keswick-bound bus could get them straight back up the road. There is little alternative to following the road uphill, as there is no access to the fellside until the top of the pass.

AMBLESIDE

Ambleside is a popular choice of base for many walkers. The narrow streets are crowded with shops offering everything from outdoor gear to giftware. There are several pubs and restaurants offering food and drink. Ambleside has good bus links with Grasmere, Keswick, Windermere, Langdale, Hawkshead and Coniston. There are also summer services over the Kirkstone Pass to Patterdale, Glenridding, Pooley Bridge and Penrith. During the summer there is also the opportunity to reach Ambleside, or leave town, via Waterhead and take a lake steamer service to Bowness or distant Lakeside. There is a Tourist Information Centre close to where the buses stop and this offers a good range of maps, guides and details of features of interest in the area.

Walkers based in Ambleside have no need for cars, as there are plenty of walks which can be accessed

High Sweden Bridge

Christine Isherwood

quickly and easily from the centre of town. Those who aren't sure of the layout of Ambleside can use prominent reference points such as the Salutation Hotel or the lovely Bridge House when trying to find their way out of town.

There are three walks described which leave Ambleside and take to the surrounding fells. One is the classic circuit around the Fairfield Horseshoe; a deservedly popular walk taking in a handful of fine summits. There is a more rugged horseshoe walk around Fairfield, while another walk wanders up through Scandale, then climbs to the top of Red Screes before following a ridge route back to Ambleside. This route includes a view of the Kirkstone Pass Inn, which is the highest pub in the Lake District. There is no need to pick a way down the steep and rocky slope to reach the pub, as the Kirkstone Pass Inn can also be reached by enjoying the walk over Wansfell, the final walk described from Ambleside. Stretched across the slopes of Wansfell is the attractive straggly village of Troutbeck, where several fine examples of vernacular architecture can be found.

In addition to all its other services, Ambleside offers a full range of accommodation options. There is a large Youth Hostel at Waterhead, several B&Bs throughout the town, and a number of large hotels. While beds can become scarce at peak periods, there are other accommodation providers in the surrounding countryside.

14 Fairfield Horseshoe

The Fairfield Horseshoe is one of the classic Lakeland fellwalks. It can be attempted from either Ambleside or Rydal. The parallel arms of the horseshoe are studded with summits which prove fairly easy to cross, although the broad, stony plateau of Fairfield does need careful route finding in poor visibility. The route is described anti-clockwise as most walkers start from Ambleside and want to get on to the fells as quickly as possible. Both Rydal and Ambleside have many features of interest if time can be spared for searching after the walk.

Distance: 10¼ miles/17km	fellwalking with some short, steep and rocky sections.
Height gain: 3,150ft/960m	
Walking time: 6 hours	**Start/Finish:** Ambleside. GR376046.
Type of walk: Moderate	

Ambleside has a confusing street pattern which first-time visitors could have difficulty following. Aim to leave the town centre by way of the Grasmere road, passing the celebrated Bridge House. Next, look out for a road on the right which is signposted for the Kirkstone Pass. Follow this narrow road and almost immediately turn left along Nook Lane. This leads past the Charlotte Mason College to reach a farmyard at Nook End Farm. Pass through the farmyard and follow the clear track beyond, crossing Low Sweden Bridge.

The track zigzags uphill and wanders into Scandale. Follow the track, but later look out for a path which heads off to the left and climbs more quickly to a higher level. The path follows a wall along the rugged crest of the fell, but sidesteps any rocky or boggy areas near the wall. Stiles are used to cross any walls running up from Scandale. Low Pike and High Pike are mere bumps on the ridge, which otherwise keeps climbing uphill in fairly easy stages.

The climbing eases for a while on the broad crest of Dove Crag. There is a summit cairn at 2,603ft/792m, but this is hardly noticed by walkers eager to reach Fairfield. Passing over Dove Crag, the ground falls away to a gap, then on the ascent of Hart Crag there is a mass of boulders and the course of the wall ends abruptly. From this point onwards, in mist, careful navigation is required. Hart Crag bears a couple of cairns on its rugged top, the highest being at 2,698ft/822m.

In clear weather it is worth picking a way along the northern edge of the fell all the way to Fairfield. There are dramatic views down a series of gullies and buttresses leading the eye along Deepdale. The top of Fairfield is a broad and stony plateau, liberally sprinkled with cairns. In mist it can be a confusing place and first-time visitors may have some difficulty spotting the summit cairn from a host of contenders. The summit cairn turns out to be the largest, and there may well be a number of people huddled against it, as Fairfield is a popular fell. The height above sea level is 2,863ft/873m.

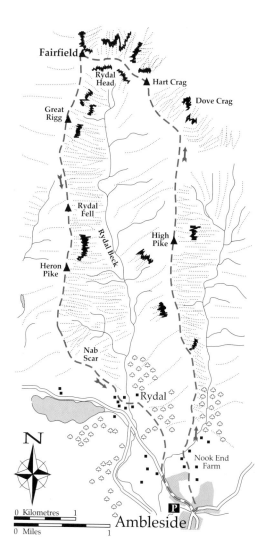

Fairfield

Rydal Head

Hart Crag

Dove Crag

Great Rigg

Rydal Fell

Rydal Beck

High Pike

Heron Pike

Nab Scar

Rydal

N

0 Kilometres 1

0 Miles 1

Nook End Farm

P

Ambleside

Views are extensive, but to be enjoyed to their best advantage it is worth scouting around the edge of the stony summit to achieve a sense of depth and perspective. The broad shoulders of the Helvellyn range effectively block any view further northwards. There is a fine prospect of the fells around Ullswater, taking in the whole of the High Street range. Looking southwards, Windermere and Coniston Water can be coaxed into the view. The Coniston and Langdale fells, Scafells and Gables, Buttermere and Newlands fells all lead the eye back round to Helvellyn.

Walk roughly southwards to leave the summit of Fairfield. In mist this needs to be done with the aid of a compass, until the clear path running towards Great Rigg is identified with certainty. Let the path lead onwards across a broad gap and up the gentle incline to the top of Great Rigg. The summit rises to a dome at 2,513ft/767m. On the descent, take care to stick to the path running along the crest of the ridge, and don't be drawn towards Stone Arthur by following the path to the right. A rather hummocky ridge extends towards Heron Pike, then the path starts to fall again towards Nab Scar.

There is a fine view over Rydal Water from Nab Scar, but there is no direct descent. A clear path heads off to the left and in places this has been reconstructed. Follow the path faithfully as it winds down the rugged slopes of rock and bracken, and it eventually leads safely to the top of the road in the little village of Rydal. Follow the road downhill, noting Wordsworth's former home of Rydal Mount off to the right, and Rydal Hall off to the left.

Many walkers return to Ambleside by walking along the main road, but there is a much more pleasant route. Look out for a signpost at an entrance to the grounds of Rydal Hall, and follow a fine track from Rydal Hall to the outskirts of Ambleside. This track stays well clear of the main road and runs through fields, leaving only a short stretch of road walking back into town.

15 Red Screes

Hordes of motorists are familiar with the sight of Red Screes even if they don't know the fell by name. It rises opposite the Kirkstone Pass Inn – the highest hostelry in the Lake District. An ascent from the Kirkstone Pass to the summit is steep and rocky throughout, while going astray on the descent could lead to serious problems. To get some distance out of the fell and stay on relatively safe ground, try an ascent from Ambleside and Scandale, and return to Ambleside along the southern ridge of the fell. It makes a delightful circuit in good weather.

Distance: 8 miles/13km	fellwalking mostly on
Height gain:	clear paths but care
2,300ft/700m	needed in mist.
Walking time: 5 hours	**Start/Finish:** Ambleside.
Type of walk: Moderate	GR376046.

Follow the Grasmere road out of the centre of Ambleside, passing the delightful curiosity called Bridge House. Look out for a turning on the right, signposted for the Kirkstone Pass. Follow this narrow road steeply uphill and pass the Golden Rule pub. Turn left into Sweden Bridge Lane and continue further uphill. A sign later confirms that this is the way to the bridge.

At the end of the narrow tarmac lane a gate leads on to a walled track. Keep walking uphill and later descend slightly as the track passes through an interesting area of delightfully mixed woodlands. Scandale Beck may be glimpsed from time to time between the trees. When the track leaves the woodland it runs close to High Sweden Bridge. Don't cross the bridge, but keep following the clear stony track onwards, further into Scandale. It runs across open ground for a while, but is soon bounded by stone walls.

Scandale Beck has to be forded at one point, which could mean wet feet in wet weather. As the path climbs up towards the head of Scandale, there is usually a wall to one side or the other, but on the final part of the climb the path pulls away from the wall and heads straight for the gap of the Scandale Pass. Cross the ladder stile on top of the pass and turn right. A path has been trodden alongside a wall which runs up a rugged fellside towards Red Screes. Follow the wall straight up the fellside until a junction of ruined walls is reached short of the top of the fell. It is necessary to head roughly eastwards across pathless ground to reach the summit trig point on Red Screes at an altitude of 2,541ft/777m.

Views from this airy perch are splendid, especially down towards Brothers Water, which is surrounded by a host of fine fells. The whole of the High Street range is well displayed, its form accentuated by a great sense of depth and perspective. The Coniston, Langdale and Scafell groups are more distant, then the eye is led across neighbouring Fairfield and along the length of the Helvellyn range. Some walkers may wish to include the celebrated Kirkstone Pass Inn in the view. This is achieved by walking to a lower viewpoint, or waiting for

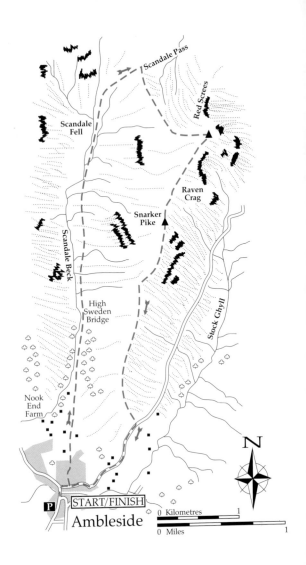

Scandale Pass

Red Screes

Scandale Fell

Raven Crag

Snarker Pike

Scandale Beck

Stock Ghyll

High Sweden Bridge

Nook End Farm

N

START/FINISH

Ambleside

0 Kilometres 1

0 Miles 1

the descent to Ambleside to begin; either way the pub will come into sight.

To descend in mist, it is best to take compass bearings, but in clear weather there should be no mistaking the start of the ridge path back to Ambleside. The path runs roughly south-west as it leaves the summit, but gradually pulls more southwards as it approaches the minor peak of Snarker Pike. Don't forget to look over the edge of Raven Crag to spot the Kirkstone Pass Inn on the way to Snarker Pike.

The path is accompanied by rather distant walls running parallel on both sides as the ground steepens beyond Snarker Pike. These two walls eventually join together, and the path crosses a ladder stile at the junction. The path is then more tightly hemmed in by walls as it continues running downhill. It finally zigzags down to join the minor road running from the Kirkstone Pass to Ambleside. Simply turn right and let the road lead straight back into Ambleside. There are some poky little streets which can be explored on the way back into the town.

16 Wansfell Pike

Wansfell Pike is not a great height, but it does have a commanding appearance above Ambleside and the head of Windermere. There is a steep climb to its summit from Ambleside, and on the far side the straggly old village of Troutbeck clings to the flank of the fell. An interesting circuit around Wansfell can be accomplished from Ambleside, visiting Troutbeck and even offering a break at the Kirkstone Pass Inn. Stock Ghyll Force also provides an entertaining little detour.

Distance: 10 miles/16km	*moderate fellwalk*
Height gain:	*followed by tracks and*
1,310ft/400m	*road walking.*
Walking time: 6 hours	**Start/Finish:** *Ambleside.*
Type of walk: A	*GR376046.*

Starting from the centre of Ambleside, locate the large Salutation Hotel and walk along a road which leads round its back. A sign on the left of this road indicates Stock Ghyll Park, which can be entered if desired. A short path wriggles through a wood, crossing footbridges and enjoying a fine waterfall. People used to pay to see this place, but now that it is free it seems that fewer people make the effort to visit it. The path rejoins the road, which is followed a little further uphill.

Look out for a ladder stile on the right side of the road, bearing a footpath sign for Troutbeck via

Wansfell. The path climbs steeply up the grassy fellside and seems to get even steeper the higher it climbs. Wansfell makes the most of what little height it possesses, and few walkers reach the top without puffing and blowing! There is another ladder stile crossing the summit fence, although the summit cairn is a disappointing heap at 1,581ft/484m.

Views are very good, especially looking along the length of Windermere. The Coniston, Langdale and Scafell ranges are lined up to the west, while most of the nearby Fairfield Horseshoe is also in view. Looking east takes in the triple tops of Froswick, Ill Bell and Yoke. More distantly, the Howgills, Yorkshire Dales and Bowland Fells can be seen.

The descent is eastwards following a clear path, then a right turn leads along the enclosed Nanny Lane. This lane twists and turns downhill and becomes quite stony before it leads on to a tarmac road at Troutbeck.

Anyone with an interest in vernacular architecture should allow plenty of extra time to work their way through Troutbeck. The village is surprisingly long and varied, stretching from Town End to Town Head and featuring some especially fine-featured structures.

To continue the walk, turn left to pass through part of Troutbeck, noting the pubs called the Mortal Man and the Queen's Head. The minor road through the village exits onto the main A592 road, where a left turn is needed. Only a short way along this road, on the right, a bridleway sign indicates a

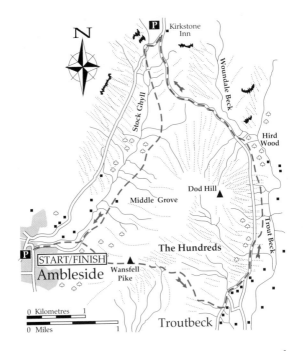

narrow path running parallel to the main road. This is Low Kingate, which stays below the level of the road and runs through delightfully wooded surroundings. There are some fine views over Troutbeck Park from it. Later, the path climbs uphill and rejoins the main road. A right turn leads onwards and upwards by road to reach the Kirkstone Pass Inn.

The Kirkstone Pass Inn is the highest Lakeland hostelry at 1,500ft/457m. Food and drink could be enjoyed at this point and there is an occasional summer bus service crossing the pass. When the time comes to depart, follow the nearby minor road which leads to Ambleside. The first steep, zigzagging stretch is known as The Struggle, though that is referring to travel in the other direction. Once a year there is a sponsored car-haul up this road, from Ambleside to the Kirkstone Pass Inn!

A footpath sign on the left of the road indicates an alternative way down to Ambleside. The path is adequately waymarked and leads past the ruins of High Grove, crossing Grove Gill on the way to the inhabited Middle Grove Farm. Follow the narrow farm access road further downhill and it leads straight back into Ambleside. The final portion was traversed on the outward journey earlier in the day, and there is again an option to admire Stock Ghyll Force in its wooded bower.

WINDERMERE

When fellwalkers think of Windermere, they think of traffic jams, crowds, ice creams and souvenirs. That may be a fair description of Windermere and neighbouring Bowness at the height of summer, but those crowds generally do not penetrate into the surrounding countryside. As many walkers are already convinced that they should be walking well away from Windermere and Bowness, the nearby countryside is often remarkably quiet.

In terms of services and facilities, Windermere and Bowness offer just about everything. There are large hotels and several B&Bs. Shops include outdoor gear retailers and souvenir sellers as well as shops offering basic food provisions. There are pubs and restaurants galore, so that food and drink is obtainable everywhere. Windermere has a rail terminus and instant access to bus services. There are buses, including open top buses in the summer, which dash between Bowness, Ambleside and Grasmere. Longer bus journeys allow places such as Kendal, Ulverston and Keswick to be reached. There are summer services which head for the Kirkstone Pass and Ullswater.

Three easy walks are described within sight of the waters of Windermere. One climbs to the celebrated viewpoint of Orrest Head, which has been praised in guidebooks written by both Wordsworth and Wainwright. This is a very short and simple walk, so the route is taken onwards in a wide circuit into relatively unfrequented countryside, nearly always in view of fine ranges of fells. When most walkers think about the Dales Way they think about the Yorkshire Dales, but the route runs all the way from Ilkley to Bowness. A stretch of the Dales Way is described as a linear walk from Staveley to Bowness, again crossing quiet countryside. The walk over Cartmel Fell is mostly confined to forests and woods, but there are open vistas and a fine view from the knobbly little fell of Gummer's How. The lovely Cartmel Fell chapel is a fine place of worship which seems deeply rooted into the fellside.

During the summer months there are opportunities to enjoy cruises on Windermere. There are several options. Some are short trips around the islands off Bowness, while others sail further and return to Bowness afterwards. The Swan, Teal and Tern operate along the full length of Windermere, linking Bowness with Ambleside and Lakeside, so that the whole of Windermere can be appreciated. It is England's longest lake and it can be busy with craft of all sorts, but there are times in winter when the waters are practically deserted.

Windermere from Rosthwaite Heights

Christine Isherwood

17 Orrest Head

Orrest Head above Windermere has long been proclaimed one of the finest viewpoints in the Lake District. It certainly offers an extensive panorama and it is very easy to reach on foot. It is all too easy and many walkers would pine for something with a bit more distance. This walk is taken beyond Orrest Head, linking paths, tracks and minor roads to explore a quiet and relatively unfrequented countryside on the doorstep of bustling Windermere. The first objective is Orrest Head, praised by poets and writers from Wordsworth to Wainwright.

Distance:
10 miles/16km
Height gain:
950ft/290m
Walking time: 5 hours
Type of walk: An easy
progression along low-level paths, tracks and roads.
Start/Finish:
Windermere railway station. GR414987.

Windermere railway station also serves as the town's bus station and has parking available nearby, as well as a busy Tourist Information Centre.

Leave the station area and cross the busy main road, keeping to the left side of the Windermere Hotel. An access road and a woodland path lead up to the bare hump of rock which is crowned with a view indicator. The ascent takes only a matter of minutes from the bustling town of Windermere.

Take in the wonderful view, storing the details in memory to compare and contrast with other viewpoints. Wordsworth described it as "a universe of Nature's fairest forms".

Looking roughly northwards from Orrest Head a white farmstead can be seen, called Causeway. A path seems to head straight towards it, but is deflected to the right of the farm to a minor road. Turn right to follow the road, then within a short while turn left through the farmyard at Near Orrest. White painted stiles and yellow arrow waymarks indicate the field path running from Near Orrest to Far Orrest. Keep to the right of Far Orrest, following signs reading "Garburn Troutbeck".

A narrow, walled lane and a track through fields lead onward to another minor road. Turn right, then left, where a sign reads: "To Kentmere via Garburn Pass". A broad, stony lane leads gradually uphill, intent on reaching the High Street fells in the distance. Save the high fells for another day, and instead look out for the prominent campsite of Limefitt Park in the valley below. When walking above the campsite, cross a stile on the right and walk uphill to cross another stile. Turn right to follow the course of another broad, stony lane. This eventually leads down past Dubbs Reservoir and runs into a tarmac road.

Bear left to follow this minor road, and keep to the left to pass other road junctions. Count off the turnings and take the third road off to the right. This road leads past Mislet Farm and continues

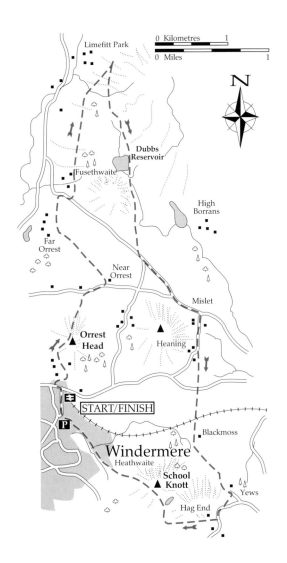

towards Heaning. Just before reaching Heaning, branch off to the left along a track and follow an access road to the busy A591 road, which needs to be crossed with care.

Straight across the main road a quiet farm road leads across a railway line, passing the farms of Blackmoss and Yews. Just after passing Yews, a path off to the right cuts a corner to reach a nearby minor road. Turn right along this road, then follow Dales Way signs on the way past Hag End Farm. Cross a gap in some low hills and descend to a gate beside a stand of four trees. Turn right to reach a small tarn, then turn left to climb to the summit of School Knott. This minor hill offers a fine view towards the end of the walk.

Leave the summit of School Knott by walking in the direction of Windermere town. A tarmac pathway is reached and this should be followed off to the right. Cross an arched bridge on the left and walk down to Droomer Drive. This residential road leads towards the centre of Windermere.

18 The Dales Way

Most keen walkers have heard of the Dales Way, but they tend to think of it in the context of the Yorkshire Dales. But this waymarked long distance walk terminates at Bowness-on-Windermere, ending with a fine panorama of Lakeland fells in the distance. The route has opened up a quiet tract of Lakeland countryside which was little explored by walkers previously. The Dales Way between Staveley and Bowness is a gentle walk, passing a few farms and crossing gently rolling hills.

Distance: 6 miles/10km
Height gain: 650ft/200m
Walking time: 3 hours
Type of walk: Easy

walking along minor roads, tracks and field paths.
Start: Staveley railway station. GR469981.

Walkers who use public transport can reach Staveley either by bus or train. Motorists could drive there, but it would be better to leave the car parked at Bowness-on-Windermere, then get the bus or train to Staveley to start the walk. Whatever option is chosen, the route starts at Staveley railway station.

Food, drink and shops are available in Staveley, then follow Station Road away from the village. This road crosses the busy A591 road using a bridge.

After crossing the bridge an access road heads off

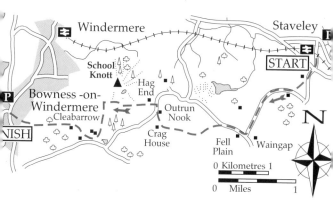

to the right to Field Close, then the Dales Way proceeds gently uphill along a path beside a wood. The path runs to a minor road near New Hall, where walkers should turn right. The road runs uphill and crosses a broad rise before descending to a junction. Turn right again to pass Fell Plain, following the road up to the brow of a hill. A track runs off to the left at this point, then the Dales Way continues along a path to reach a small plantation. Keep the plantation to the right and walk around it, then head off to the left to cross a shallow valley, aiming for Crag House.

Turn right at Crag House, leaving the farm access road to follow a field path to Outrun Nook. Continue along another minor road, then head left on the farm access road to Hag End. Pass through the farmyard and look ahead to spot a stile. The way forward becomes vague, but head up into a shallow valley and pass through a gap in the hills. Walk down towards a gate beside four trees.

Turn left at the gate beside the trees and follow a track downhill. Turn left onto another track and follow this down to a road. Turn right to follow the road a short way, then turn right again and head towards Cleabarrow. Follow the access road towards Cleabarrow, but head off to the left along a path before reaching the building. This path runs across a minor road near Matson Ground. Continue straight ahead to one side of another access road, then follow a track close to the slopes of Brant Fell. After crossing another access road there is a good view of Windermere below.

A stone seat has been dedicated to Dales Wayfarers and no doubt a short rest would be permitted for those who had walked only a short part of the route. Enjoy the views, which are richly wooded with the higher fells appearing only in the distance.

A path runs straight down a steep slope and the walk continues down Brantfell Road. Bear left through the popular resort of Bowness-on-Windermere to reach Bowness Pier. Walkers who still have a few crumbs left over from their packed lunches can feed the swans, ducks and raucous gulls which have a habit of congregating along the lake shore.

19 Cartmel Fell

Cartmel Fell is a rugged, wooded tract of countryside between the southern reaches of Windermere and the River Winster. The woods include both deciduous and coniferous stands, as coppicing for posts, bobbins and charcoal gave way to forests offering a quicker return. The tree cover smooths out the hummocky nature of these low fells and hides small tarns and pools from sight. Fell Foot is the most popular visitor site, while Gummer's How offers the finest views. A mixture of paths and tracks lead to Cartmel Fell chapel and back.

Distance:
8 miles/13km
Height gain:
1,475ft/450m
Walking time: 5 hours
Type of walk: Generally
easy tracks and paths through woodlands and rough pasture.
Start/Finish: Fell Foot Country Park. GR381867.

There is an occasional bus service passing Fell Foot Country Park and there is abundant parking for cars. Very occasionally, there is a ferry service linking Fell Foot with Lakeside, in case any walkers arrive on one of the Lakeside steamers. If this final option is to be considered, consult the timetables to be sure of a connection. Fell Foot is a popular little country park on the shore of Windermere. It includes a restaurant, although this is only likely to be open when the place is busy.

Leave Fell Foot and cross the main road, then take the steep minor road uphill which is signposted for Cartmel Fell. The road climbs up alongside a forest and eventually passes a small roadside parking space. There is a gate on the left which gives access to a path leading to Gummer's How. Note before setting off that this path leads only to the summit of Gummer's How, and that a return needs to be made back to the road. The path is clear and obvious throughout, but becomes very steep before the summit trig point is reached at 1,054ft/321m.

The view from this minor height is really quite extensive. The length of Windermere can be observed, with many prominent Lakeland fells arranged in an arc from Black Combe to the Shap Fells. The Coniston Fells and the fells around Ambleside are well displayed, while more distantly the Howgills, Yorkshire Dales and Bowland Fells can be distinguished.

When the view has been sampled, turn around and walk back down the path to return to the road. Turn left to cross the final rise on the minor road, then turn right along a road signposted as being unsuitable for cars. This lane leads to Sow How. Walk through the farmyard, then turn left along a bridleway which can be rather muddy. Follow this track past the small pool of Sow How Tarn, crossing the outflow beneath a small dam. Climb uphill a short way, following the bridleway arrows over a rise and down through a wood to an old barn. A path rises over the rugged top of Raven's Barrow then begins to run more and more steeply down to a minor road.

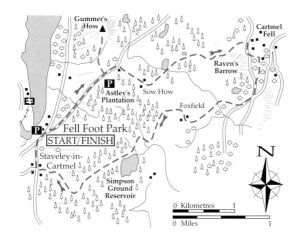

Turn right along the road, then left to locate
Cartmel Fell chapel. This low structure is virtually
hidden from view behind a screen of trees, but it is
worth searching for and proves to be a treasure
store of history. Also known as St. Anthony's, the
church has been used for worship since 1504. It
was built as a chapel-of-ease and was tied to
Cartmel Priory. It somehow escaped brutal
restoration and contains some interesting details.
When the building has been inspected, walk away
from it along its path, cross over a road and
continue straight onwards through a wood. A
narrow, bracken-covered path leads to another
minor road, where a left turn leads to a road
junction. Turn right as signposted for High
Newton.

A footpath sign on the right indicates Lakeside.
Walk through three gates before turning left along

a track, then turn right along the access road passing the farm at Foxfield. When the tarmac surface expires at a gate, turn left to follow a path signposted up a grassy hillside. Turn left along the edge of a forest, looking out for a waymark which shows a right turn leading into the trees. This path runs to Simpson Ground Reservoir, where it is necessary to keep to the right to pass the dam. Follow a path near the shore until it heads off into the trees. A forest road later runs downhill.

Leave the forest road by following a path off to the right. This runs down through the trees and enters a large sloping field. Cross over this field and go through a gate at its lower end. A farm road runs down to the village of Staveley, where a right turn along the road leads back towards the Fell Foot Country Park.

KENTMERE

Kentmere and Longsleddale are served by narrow, twisting, dead-end minor roads. This should help to protect and preserve them from unsightly development and large-scale tourism projects. Many motorists who would consider that they knew their way around Lakeland would be at a loss to reach Kentmere or Longsleddale without the aid of a map. There are many walkers who reach Kentmere from Troutbeck, or Longsleddale from Mardale, rather than drive along the narrow roads serving either of the dales.

One walk is described around Kentmere and another around Longsleddale. They are both horseshoe walks and as they lie side by side they have one ridge in common. This is no bad thing, for the ridge is well worth walking twice. The

Donald Dakeyne

Green Quarter, Kentmere

Kentmere Horseshoe is well on its way to being regarded as a classic Lakeland horseshoe walk. The triple summits of Yoke, Ill Bell and Froswick are crossed on one side of the round, while Mardale Ill Bell stands at the head. Harter Fell, Kentmere Pike and Shipman Knotts complete the circuit before the final descent into the dale. The Longsleddale round takes in Shipman Knotts, Kentmere Pike and Harter Fell, then crosses the Gatesgarth Pass and crosses the lonely summit of Tarn Crag before a steep and rocky descent back into the dale.

There are few facilities in these two remote dales. There is barely a cup of tea or a bed to be had, although once the lower parts of the dales are reached there are more services. Kendal and Staveley are the nearest places offering a choice of accommodation, shops, pubs, food, drink and bus services. Motorists will find that parking at both Kentmere and Sadgill is extremely limited. Great care must be taken to park as tidily as possible. This not only leaves access for farm vehicles, but also facilitates anyone else needing a parking space. In these out of the way places, it is very important for visitors to maintain good relations with the dalesfolk. There is an occasional summer bus service to Kentmere.

20 Kentmere Horseshoe

The walk around the head of Kentmere is one of the classic horseshoe walks of the Lake District. It embraces two ridges of fine fells which extend southwards from High Street. The walk is conveniently begun from the village of Kentmere, which is an interesting little settlement even if it is short on facilities for tired, hungry and thirsty walkers. Route finding on the tops is generally easy, but in mist a little more care is needed and it should be remembered that many of the fells around Kentmere have steep and rocky flanks.

Distance: 12 miles/20km
Height gain: 3,500ft/1,050m
Walking time: 8 hours
Type of walk: A rugged fellwalk which is mostly accomplished on good paths.
Start/Finish: Kentmere Church. GR456041.

Even before the village of Staveley was bypassed there were few who were aware that the only road serving Kentmere began at that point. Many fellwalkers cover the Kentmere Horseshoe from neighbouring Troutbeck, which involves climbing on to the Garburn Pass twice during the day's walk. Those who do drive into Kentmere will find a long and narrow road leads towards the dale head. Parking is extremely limited, with a space near the church in the village of Kentmere and more spaces available for a small donation at the cottage called

The Nook. There is an occasional summer bus service to Kentmere.

Starting the walk from the church, continue uphill to pass The Nook and set off along the rough and stony bridleway towards the Garburn Pass. The small fields around Kentmere village are quickly left behind and the track climbs uphill across the rugged fellside and is clear and obvious throughout. On reaching the top of the Garburn Pass there is a view across Troutbeck which takes in ranks of fine Lakeland fells. Many more will be seen before the day's walk is completed.

Turn right to leave the top of the Garburn Pass. A path can be followed alongside a wall which runs very roughly northwards along the crest of the fell. There are some rather wet and muddy stretches which the path attempts to outflank. Firmer footing is gained as the ascent begins in earnest and there are protruding rocks after the wall runs out on the shoulder of Yoke. The summit of Yoke is the first 'nail' in the Kentmere Horseshoe, with a cairn on top standing at 2,309ft/706m. In mist, note that there is a path which narrowly misses the summit cairn.

There is a gentle descent to a gap in the fells, then a short and steep pull up onto the domed summit of Ill Bell. Cairns have a habit of coming and going on this rocky felltop, as visitors are continually raising them and knocking them down. The highest point on the fell is at 2,476ft/757m. Again, as on Yoke, there is a path which cuts across the fellside and completely avoids the summit.

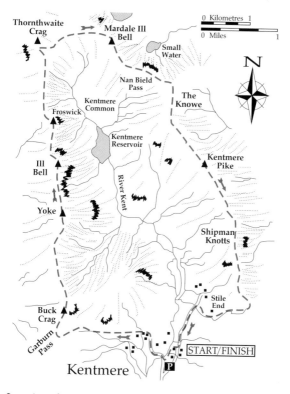

Thornthwaite Crag
Mardale Ill Bell
Small Water
Nan Bield Pass
The Knowe
Kentmere Common
Froswick
Kentmere Reservoir
Kentmere Pike
Ill Bell
River Kent
Yoke
Shipman Knotts
Buck Crag
Stile End
Garburn Pass
START/FINISH
Kentmere

Leaving the top of Ill Bell a path drops steeply to a narrow gap, then a ridge can be followed more gently uphill to reach the top of Froswick. The summit cairn on Froswick is perched at 2,359ft/720m. This trio of fine fells crossed so early in the walk around Kentmere proves to be a fine romp in clear weather.

Looking straight ahead, a path can be seen

113

climbing towards Thornthwaite Crag and ultimately heading towards High Street. There is no need to include those two summits in the walk around the Kentmere Horseshoe. A path branches off to the right before the top of Thornthwaite Crag, and it altogether misses out the broad summit of High Street. The next objective becomes Mardale Ill Bell. There is very little climbing onto the top of the fell, which is really no more than a rugged hump appended to the flank of High Street. The highest point reaches 2,496ft/761m and bears a couple of cairns. Views over the edge take in Blea Water and Mardale, and furnish perhaps a more interesting sight than that of distant fells.

The path continues beyond the summit of Mardale Ill Bell and becomes steeper and rockier as it descends to the top of the Nan Bield Pass.

"Bield" is the name given to a shelter, and a stout wall shelter has been constructed on top of the pass. Walkers who know they are running short of time or energy can exit southwards from the Nan Bield Pass and follow a long path and track back to the village of Kentmere. Those who are still game for some fine fellwalking should climb straight up the steep and rocky slopes of Harter Fell. The gradient eases towards the top and the summit cairn is truly weird – boulders and rusty old fenceposts have been heaped into a strange construction on top of the fell at 2,539ft/778m.

Harter Fell is the highest summit gained on the walk around the Kentmere Horseshoe, and it presents a fine vista in clear weather, taking in sights as distant as the

Pennines and Morecambe Bay. The broad summit area cuts out good views of the dales, but by scouting around the plateau there are places where a real sense of depth can be brought into the view. Looking back across the Nan Bield Pass, the Coniston, Langdale, Scafell, Buttermere and Helvellyn fells can be seen. The nearby broad shoulders of High Street take up a sizeable wedge of the view. Walking northwards allows for a splendid view of Mardale. The way off the top of Harter Fell is roughly southwards.

Follow the line of a fence southwards to the minor bump of The Knowe, then drift more to the south-east across a peaty gap around Brown Howe. The course of an old wall is encountered and this provides a faithful guide over Kentmere Pike in mist. The summit rises to 2,397ft/730m. The ground falls away further south-east and there is later a bifurcation in the path being followed. Heading off to the right gives an early, rugged descent into Kentmere. It is worth keeping to the left, however, to take in the hummocky crest of Shipman Knotts. There is only minimal climbing to the summit, which stands at 1,926ft/587m. This is the final 'nail' in the course of the Kentmere Horseshoe.

A wall leading along the rugged crest of Shipman Knotts provides a good guide downhill. There is some rocky ground at first, then the slope is fairly gentle for a short while, before a final steep descent to the top of a pass. Turn right to follow a clear track downhill to Stile End. Turn left to follow the narrow road down through the dale bottom, remembering to keep bearing right to return to Kentmere village.

21 Longsleddale

Longsleddale is something of a lost Lakeland dale. It has its devotees, but most fellwalkers don't go there and wouldn't have a clue how to get there by car. The journey into Longsleddale begins near Kendal, and the narrow, winding road needs care from beginning to end. There is a fine horseshoe walk around Longsleddale. Half of the route is coincident with the Kentmere Horseshoe, while the other half is wild, rugged and unfrequented. The tiny hamlet of Sadgill is where the walk begins and ends.

Distance: *9 miles/14km*
Height gain: *2,625ft/800m*
Walking time: *5 hours*
Type of walk: *A rugged*
fellwalk with some good paths and a final very steep descent.
Start/Finish: *Sadgill. GR483057.*

Sadgill is literally the end of the road in Longsleddale. There is a clear track proceeding further, but most motorists would not wish to test their suspension on it. Cars are usually parked in a space before reaching the final bridge.

The walk starts by crossing the bridge over the River Sprint at Sadgill. A clear track heads off to the left of the buildings, picking its way across a wooded fellside before reaching more open ground. This is the course of the old road which ran over to Kentmere and Troutbeck.

There is a cairn on top of the pass, and at that point turn right and start following a wall up the rugged fellside. The ground steepens, but taken steadily the slope presents no problems. Eventually, the rocky summit of Shipman Knotts is gained at 1,926ft/587m. There is a good path continuing along the crest and the next summit of note is Kentmere Pike, whose rounded form rises to an altitude of 2,397ft/730m. A wall forms a useful guide over the top in mist and there is a peaty depression to be crossed further along the crest of the fell. The ground rises again and the course of a fence leads to the top of Harter Fell. There is a strange cairn composed of boulders and rusty iron fenceposts at 2,539ft/778m.

Harter Fell is a fine viewpoint, taking in all the fells around Kentmere, Longsleddale and Mardale. More distant ranges of Lakeland fells can also be observed, while in clear weather the view extends towards the Pennines and Morecambe Bay.

The Longsleddale round continues by following the fence north-east from the summit of Harter Fell, and a slight detour away from the fence allows a fine view down into the depths of Mardale.

The fence runs down towards the minor hump of Adam Seat. It isn't necessary to walk onto the hump, as there is a path branching off to the left running more directly to the top of Gatescarth Pass than the line taken by the fence. Go through the gate on the top of the pass. Some walkers may wish to complete a "pure" horseshoe walk by following the fence straight up the steep slope of Branstree,

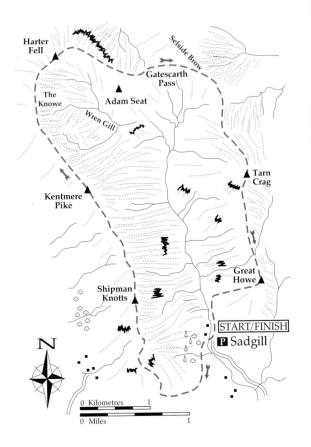

but this fell can be omitted from the round. Instead, contour across the fellside roughly eastwards and aim for the broad and boggy gap between Branstree and Tarn Crag. Another gate in another fence will be reached on the gap.

The fence can be followed southwards to commence the ascent of Tarn Crag. The slope is generally easy, although there are some boggy areas which may need to be sidestepped.

The summit of Tarn Crag appears, at first sight, to be crowned with a monumental cairn at 2,176ft/664m. On closer inspection the structure is found to be a most formidable piece of work and not a cairn at all. It is one of a handful of survey points built over the fells from Haweswater to Longsleddale. They were all connected by a line of sight and measurements taken over the top of the fell were used by engineers tunnelling beneath the fell to construct an aqueduct carrying water from Haweswater southwards to Manchester. Each of the stone structures had a wooden dais and rotting timbers from this can be distinguished around the base of the column. Looking back and forth, it is possible to discern one more column on Great Howe and one on the slopes of Branstree.

Head roughly southwards from the top of Tarn Crag to approach the survey point on Great Howe. The ground underfoot is pathless and rough. There is bog and tough vegetation to cross, as well as a fence and a small beck. The column on Great Howe is not exactly on the crest of the fell, but there are fine views along the length of Longsleddale nonetheless.

Leave the column and head roughly westwards to reach the top of a very steep and rugged slope. This is the start of a descent which needs to be taken carefully. Look across the fellside to spot the course of a fence and wall running straight down the fellside. Pick a way carefully towards this feature and follow it gingerly downhill. The aim is to reach the track running along the floor of Longsleddale. When this has been safely accomplished, turn left and follow it back to the space where cars are usually parked.

Facilities in Longsleddale are extremely limited. There might be a chance to obtain teas and snacks near Sadgill, but if they are not available, then drive out of the dale and head for Kendal, which has a full range of services for the tired, hungry and thirsty walker.

SHAP FELLS

The Shap Fells must be one of the least walked parts of the Lake District. Shap village is a long, straggly, utilitarian sort of place, but does possess accommodation, food and drink. It is a major staging post on the celebrated Coast to Coast Walk. Hence, there are some parts of some of the walks described which may feature heavily-laden walkers.

There are two walks offered over the Shap Fells. The Shap Fells themselves are an area of rolling moorlands and high pastures. Walkers who study their maps closely will be surprised to discover names such as Borrowdale and Wasdale, but these are not to be confused with the famous counterparts away over to the west.

One walk takes in the moorland hump of Wasdale Pike, crossing the sprawling Great Yarlside before picking a way down through Sleddale to pass Wet Sleddale Reservoir. The road through Shap used to carry constant traffic, although that has practically all been transferred to the M6 motorway. The area has interesting historic and prehistoric remains which can be discovered on an easy walking route.

The final walk is more akin to fellwalking, and takes in the forgotten dale of Swindale. There is a fine circuit which takes in Selside Pike and Branstree, overlooking Mardale, before a long descent through Mosedale and Swindale. This route also includes a track known as the Corpse

Road, recalling how the deceased of Mardale and Swindale once had to be packed out to Shap for burial.

Those in search of accommodation, pubs and shops close to these three walks will naturally settle on Shap. It is possible to be based somewhere else and commute backwards and forwards by car. Public transport is limited to occasional buses to Shap, and nothing at all to out of the way places such as Swindale.

Some would say that the Shap Fells were for connoisseurs of quiet countryside, while others might be less impressed and hasten to get to somewhere that was rockier and busier.

22 Shap Fells

The Shap Fells are well off the beaten track as far as most walkers are concerned, but they are becoming more and more well known. The walk offered here makes a complete circuit of the hills and moorlands around Wet Sleddale. The dale has been flooded by a reservoir, but this is apparent only towards the end of the walk. Most of the time, the scene is of barren upland moorlands, and a detour to Harrop Pike is necessary to bring a good range of fells into view. Fences form a useful aid to navigation on this walk.

Distance:
15 miles/24km
Height gain:
1,640ft/500m
Walking time: *8 hours*
Type of walk: *Rugged*

moorlands with some good paths and tracks in places.
Start/Finish: *Wet Sleddale Reservoir. GR555115.*

Wet Sleddale is signposted from the A6 road south of Shap and has surprisingly good access from the M6 motorway. Follow the narrow road towards the reservoir and park close to the dam. Walk back down the road from the reservoir, until just before a junction with another narrow road. Turn right to follow a field path which passes a large building and reaches the A6 road close to a small dam. Cross the road and turn right, then turn left along a track entering the Shap Blue Quarry. Numerous signposts mark the course of the public footpath through this site, with a request to "keep to side" to avoid lorries and trucks. The Shap Blue Quarry has a yard full of concrete pipeworks and an array of stone-crushing machinery.

The right of way leaves the top side of the quarry and follows a fine grassy track over a rise. There is a gradual descent to pass through a sheep pen and cross a farm access road, then the track climbs uphill again and eventually joins the A6 road at a high crest. Turn left along the A6 and follow it downhill through a small forest. Emerging from the trees, look out for a right turn where a sign announces the Shap Pink Quarry. The access road for the quarry is based on an old track leading to Wasdale Head Farm. Avoid the quarry and keep low to follow the track towards the derelict farm.

A gateway is reached just before the farm. Head off to the right and follow a drystone wall uphill and across a rugged slope. Next, follow the line of a fence uphill, passing a number of large granite boulders. There is a junction with another fence, and beyond this point it is best to gain height and head straight for the crest of the rugged moorland. Tough heather needs to be crossed, but the walking gets easier after passing a cairn on the minor summit of Wasdale Pike. Continuing further along the moorland crest, twin grooves made by wheeled vehicles will be encountered and following these offers easier walking onwards and upwards. After passing a gateway, a fence and track pursue parallel courses onto the top of Great Yarlside.

Turn right on Great Yarlside to follow another

fence which crosses a broad moorland gap. On the next gentle ascent, there is a gate in another fence. Beyond can be seen the prominent cairn on the summit of Harrop Pike at 2,090ft/637m. It is worth following the fence up to that point to obtain the best views of the day.

In clear weather, the expanse of Morecambe Bay is followed by Black Combe and the Coniston Fells. The High Street range takes up practically all of the nearest scene, while further afield are the North Pennines, Howgills and Yorkshire Dales.

Retrace steps back alongside the fence, go through the gate, then turn left. A fence can be followed down a rough, grassy, boggy moorland slope and across a broad gap. When the fence starts rising slightly, look out for a track coming through a gateway. It crosses from Mosedale to Wet Sleddale, rising slightly on the southern slopes of High Wether Howe. Turn right to follow this track towards Wet Sleddale. After a slight rise the grassy track falls gently and eventually passes a gateway in a wall. Continue along the track, passing a couple more gateways and enjoying widening views across Wet Sleddale Reservoir. When the track emerges from the walled enclosures and reaches open country again, follow a wall onwards and downhill in the direction of Shap.

A small plantation is passed, just across the line of the wall. After passing it, look out for a gate on the right marked with a small "footpath" notice. A grassy track can be followed down through fields to a barn, where a right turn leads along another track. This track drops down onto a minor road close to Sleddale Grange. Turn left to follow the road, passing above the reservoir dam and gradually running downhill. After passing Thorney Bank, look out for a footbridge spanning the River Lowther and cross it to reach another minor road on the other side. Turn right and this road leads back to the dam and car park.

The nearest facilities for tired, hungry and thirsty walkers are at Shap. There are pubs, shops and accommodation options, as well as an occasional bus service to Penrith. Walkers travelling without a car could base themselves at Shap and would still be able to complete this circuit at the cost of a little extra distance.

23 Swindale

Swindale is seldom visited by fellwalkers, although it is a rugged and remote dale with plenty of interesting sights. It is deemed to be too far off the beaten track and is therefore left mostly to walkers living in nearby places such as Penrith and Kendal. There is a fine circuit available which takes in an old Corpse Road, a couple of quiet summits, a long and empty dale, and some striking waterfalls; it is rare to meet anyone else in the area.

Distance: 10 miles/16km
Height gain: 1,740ft/530m
Walking time: 6 hours
Type of walk: Mostly rugged moorland walking with some useful fences and paths.
Start/Finish: Swindale Foot. GR522142.

The Swindale road is very narrow and has no real space to accommodate cars. Park near Swindale Foot, off the road near a cattle grid, where a small sign points out that there is no parking on the road ahead.

Continue along the road on foot, passing Swindale Foot, a small waterworks dam and Truss Gap, to reach the end of the road at the farmstead of Swindale Head. The road walk, although unavoidable, is pleasant enough.

Go through a gate at Swindale Head and immediately turn right to start climbing uphill. There is a footpath sign for the Corpse Road,

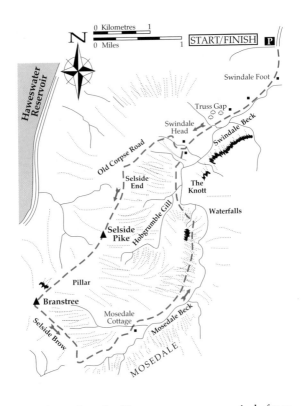

recalling that bodies were once carried from Mardale, through Swindale, for burial at Shap. On the first stage of the ascent, turn right to go through a small gate and cross over a beck. A broad track flanked by gorse bushes climbs further uphill in zigzags and crosses a higher part of the beck. A grassy path continues at a more gentle gradient across the moorland beyond, and there are cairns and posts which help to keep walkers on course.

Just before reaching the highest part of the old Corpse Road, look out for another grassy path which heads off to the left. Follow this uphill and enjoy the unfolding views towards the High Street range, Mardale and Haweswater. Keep climbing along the path, vague in some places, to reach a large summit cairn on Selside Pike at 2,142ft/655m.

The height of the fell militates against it being a good Lakeland viewpoint, for the High Street range dominates to the west. Eastwards, however, a long stretch of the Pennines is in view across the broad Vale of Eden.

Follow the fence roughly south-westwards away from the summit of Selside Pike. It wasn't stretched along the crest of these fells, but was drawn off to one side. Its course is something of a roller-coaster ride. First there is a downhill stretch, then a rise uphill, then down again, then finally a longer pull up the slopes of Branstree.

Off to the left, a tall survey column will be visible, which was linked with other columns in these fells on a line-of-sight basis. Measurements taken over the top of these fells determined the course of a tunnel beneath the fells to carry water southwards from Haweswater to Manchester. The top of Branstree features a junction of a fence and a wall at 2,333ft/713m. Despite having gained extra height since leaving Selside Pike, the view improves very little, although the lofty Scafells can be seen poking their heads above the High Street range.

Cross the fence on top of Branstree to leave the summit and follow the course of the stout stone wall downhill. The wall expires on the way and a stretch of fencing leads onwards onto a broad and boggy moorland gap. There is a gate on this gap, and by passing through it walkers can begin the descent through Mosedale.

There are a number of Mosedales in the Lake District and they are all broad and boggy places. This Mosedale conforms to the rule.

There is a path of sorts down through the dale, but it is vague in places and it is always a good idea to try and pick out its line in the view ahead. In some places the path may braid and rejoin later. The first feature of note to look out for is Mosedale Cottage. This is situated against the fellside near some old slate quarry spoil. The cottage is left open as a bothy and seems to be well used and cared for.

Follow a clear track away from the cottage, passing through gates at either side of a large enclosure. The track becomes vague again later, but keeping to the left generally allows its course to be spotted easily. Generally, the track sticks to the fellside where there is a firmer footing. Paths leading out onto the boggy floor of the dale are not good to follow.

A fine zigzag path later leads downhill on a steeper and rockier slope. There are some waterfalls off to the right, worth a visit if time can be spared. The path runs out onto the floor of Swindale, where a good track leads towards a bridge. A gated track runs back towards the farmstead at Swindale Head, which was passed earlier in the day. All that remains is to walk back along the narrow road from Swindale Head to Swindale Foot to return to the space where cars can be parked.

HAWESWATER

There was once a lovely lake called Haweswater in a lovely dale called Mardale, where the few walkers who ventured into the fells would retire in the evening to the Dun Bull at Mardale Green. All that changed in the 1930s when a dam was built and the level of Haweswater was raised. The reservoir of Haweswater takes up much more of the dale than did the original lake. The tell-tale sterile rim around the reservoir occurs whenever distant Manchester makes heavy demands on the impounded water. The tiny village at Mardale Green, along with its pub and church, were demolished to make way for the reservoir.

Originally, permission was sought to exclude walkers from the catchment area of Haweswater, which is a substantial tract of countryside. However, the position has been practically reversed and the water authorities have aided the construction of a footpath entirely encircling Haweswater. This is the first of three routes in the area. The Haweswater shore walk can be quite scenic when the weather is fine and the level of the water is high. Even when the level falls low, there is always the chance that the ruins of former buildings and field boundaries might emerge at the dale head.

Another walk heads for the heights, climbing onto High Street and making a skyline traverse towards Harter Fell. The Mardale Horseshoe includes some rugged ridges and features some fine views from the fells. The other walk in this section is likely to be very quiet. Old paths and tracks are linked on a circuit around Bampton Common, where few walkers venture.

Following the demolition of the Dun Bull in Mardale, the Haweswater Hotel was built alongside the new reservoir. This is the only place offering accommodation, food and drink in Mardale. Those wishing to stay, eat or drink anywhere else will need to head for Bampton, Shap or Askham, if not further afield. Nor are there any helpful services such as buses, although there is an occasional minibus service between Burnbanks and Penrith.

24 Around Haweswater

Haweswater is not really a lake but a reservoir whose water is piped to distant Manchester. The dam was raised during the 1930s and considerably extended the size of the original lake. As a result, the fellsides flanking Haweswater fall steeply into the lake and there are no level pastures remaining in the dale. A tiny village at Mardale Green, with a church and pub, was levelled and consigned to the depths. It occasionally emerges during drought years and can be overlooked from the path which encircles the reservoir.

Distance:
10 miles/16km
Height gain:
330ft/100m
Walking time: 5 hours
Type of walk: An easy

circuit around the shores of a reservoir with a few rough stretches.
Start/Finish: Mardale Head Car Park. GR469107.

Several minor roads have to be successfully linked to reach the car park at the head of Haweswater. Tall fells frown on Mardale Head and in recent years the area has become the haunt of golden eagles. The presence of the eagles is readily indicated by a crowded car park and a large number of birdwatchers carrying an array of powerful optical instruments. If a space can be secured in the car park, then the walk can begin. The route comes in two distinct halves. First, there is a path which exploits the narrow strip of land between the shore of

Haweswater and the approach road. The second half of the walk crosses a rugged fellside to return to the dalehead.

Route directions are hardly necessary most of the way, but start by picking up the line of the path between the road and the shore. Follow the path onwards, noting that it was specially constructed for walkers. Footbridges have been installed over inflowing becks to make progress easier. When Haweswater is full there is a small island in view off the end of The Rigg, called Wood Howe. When the level is low, vast expanses of mud are revealed and the island becomes joined to the fellside. The ruins of Mardale Green become exposed, along with tumbled drystone walls and lanes. Along with the eagles, the sight of the drowned village can cause a build-up of traffic on the Haweswater road.

The next feature of note is an ornamental tower with its foundations deep in the water. This is the draw-off tower, where water leaves Haweswater to slake the thirst of Manchester. There is an aqueduct underneath the fells which was tunnelled through to Longsleddale. The tower contains some stonework from the church which once stood at Mardale Head. A short way beyond the tower, but not obvious from the line of the path, is the Haweswater Hotel. This place offers accommodation, food and drink. It was built to replace the Dun Bull which was levelled and submerged at Mardale Green.

The path continues along the narrow strip between the road and the shore and eventually reaches a boathouse. The minor road has to be followed past the dam of Haweswater. Note that

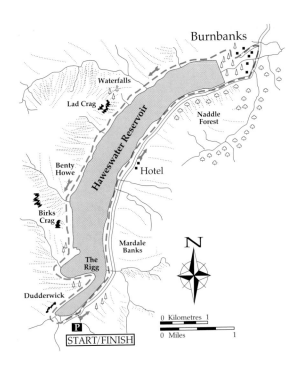

there is no access to the dam, although it can be seen between trees. Follow the road downhill and cross Naddle Bridge. Immediately on the left is a footpath leading up to the waterworks village of Burnbanks. Keep left to pass through the village, walking past the dam again to regain the shore path.

A fellside track is signposted from Burnbanks which returns towards Mardale Head on the more rugged side of Haweswater. For the most part the path runs fairly high above the shore, and narrow belts of trees sometimes obscure a view of the water. There is a significant break in the line of trees where the torrents of Measand Falls pour down the fellside into Haweswater.

The further along the shore the path proceeds, the narrower it becomes. There is one stretch which climbs high above the water, then there is a descent into Riggindale in the shadow of High Street. There are two alternative routes onwards. One is to follow the shore faithfully through the small forest on the point of The Rigg, while the other is to climb over The Rigg without entering the forest. Either way, there is only a short walk along a narrow arm of Haweswater to bring the circuit to a close. The car park at Mardale Head is clearly in view and is reached by following a path across the head of the dale.

25 High Street

The High Street range appears deceptively smooth in many distant views. On closer acquaintance it is found to have very steep flanks, a number of fine corries and some places where immense rocky crags are evident. The Mardale flank of High Street is particularly rugged and features cliff-girt corries and rocky ridges. There is a splendid horseshoe walk around the head of Mardale, and if Mardale was in a busier part of Lakeland the circuit would be very well known.

Distance:
7¼ miles/12km
Height gain:
2,430ft/740m
Walking time: 4 hours
Type of walk: Rugged
fellwalking with several clear paths and some steep slopes.
Start/Finish: *Mardale Head car park.*
GR469107.

Leave the car park at Mardale Head and follow a path straight across the level dalehead. Turn right to follow the shore of Haweswater, although this "arm" of the reservoir may sometimes be no more than a mudflat in a dry year.

Don't walk into the forest on the end of The Rigg, but follow the path uphill onto the crest of the ridge. Turn left and start following a wall along the rugged crest in the direction of High Street. Rough Crag and Riggindale Crag provide a fine walk towards High Street. Once the initial steep pull is accomplished, there is easier walking and fine views into the flanking dales. There is a steep pull up Long Stile to gain the broad top of High Street. Walk straight onwards to reach the wall which crosses High Street, then turn left to gain the trig point at 2,718ft/828m.

High Street may indeed be high, but its broad shoulders do not allow for very good views. Extensive, certainly, but only by scouting around the edges of the grassy summit can a real sense of depth be gained. Distant views embrace the North Pennines, Howgills and Yorkshire Dales, while closer to hand are the Shap Fells. Morecambe Bay lies southwards. The Coniston, Langdale, Scafell and Fairfield groups fill the western skyline, then the Helvellyn and Skiddaw fells continue round to the north.

In mist it might be tempting to hug the fell wall and follow its course southwards from the trig point on High Street. But this can be done only for a few paces before it is necessary to drift leftwards away from the wall. Follow a path running towards the hummocky top of Mardale Ill Bell.

In clear weather, there are dramatic views over the edge of High Street and Mardale Ill Bell towards the dark, deep pool of Blea Water. Mardale Ill Bell bears a couple of cairns, the highest standing at 2,496ft/761m.

The path continues beyond the summit of Mardale Ill Bell, becoming steeper and rockier as it drops down to the top of the Nan Bield Pass. The name "Bield" is given to any type of shelter and there is a stout wall shelter on top of the pass. Walkers who

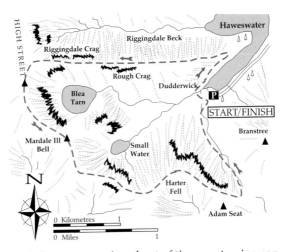

think they are running short of time or stamina can exit northwards from the Nan Bield Pass and follow a steep and stony path by way of Small Water to return to Mardale Head. Those who know they are able for more fellwalking should climb straight up the steep and rocky slopes of Harter Fell. The gradient becomes gentler near the top and the summit cairn proves to be very strange. A heap of boulders and rusty fenceposts have been fashioned into a strange construction at 2,539ft/778m on top of the fell.

Harter Fell offers a very good view in clear weather, although like neighbouring High Street it has a broad and grassy summit which cuts out views into the surrounding dales. By walking around the rim of the broad summit the views feature a fine sense of depth.

Walking northwards along the line of a fence

commences the descent, and a slight detour away from it allows a fabulous view into Mardale. The fence changes direction and offers a sure guide all the way down from Harter Fell to the top of the Gatescarth Pass. On the lower slopes there is no need to follow the fence across the hump of Adam Seat, as a path leads off to the left and drops more directly onto the Gatescarth Pass.

Purists might like to include the summit of Branstree in the circuit around Mardale, but that would leave a very steep and tedious descent to Mardale Head. For an easy descent from the fells, simply turn left on the Gatescarth Pass and let the clear, stony track lead downhill. The track runs all the way back to the car park at Mardale Head.

26 Bampton Common

The eastern fringes of the Lake District were seldom visited in the past, but more and more walkers are exploring the area. Even recently, it would have been unusual to meet anyone on the field paths around Bampton, or on the broad moorlands of Bampton Common, but now it is likely that at least a couple of other walkers would be spotted. This walk starts in Bampton and heads around Bampton Common. It includes the top of Wether Hill on the course of the High Street Roman road.

Distance: 10 miles/16km	used paths and tracks
Height gain:	which need careful
1,800ft/550m	navigation in mist.
Walking time: 6 hours	**Start/Finish:** Bampton.
Type of walk: Little	GR515183.

There is very little space to park a car in or near Bampton. If walkers are patronising the inns or B&Bs in either Bampton or Bampton Grange, then they may be permitted to park their cars for the day. Whatever happens, do not leave the car where it causes an obstruction or inconvenience.

Leave Bampton as if heading for Penrith, but turn left at a telephone box, cross a cattle grid and follow a fell road steeply uphill. The terrain alongside the road is surprisingly rugged considering that the walk has only just started. A farm is passed, then the road makes a zigzag uphill and crosses another cattle grid. Look out for a footpath sign on the right and take care to negotiate the field path with careful reference to a map. There are markers showing the way to stiles and gates at first. The path is not well trodden, but passes below a pair of barns, then keeps just above a farmhouse at Skews.

The continuation of the path is clear at first, following a grassy track through gateways. There is the wooded Gill Beck to cross using a footbridge, then the route climbs towards another farm. Keep to the left of the farm buildings before entering the farmyard. There is a small gate, then a larger gate to pass through, before a wall is followed roughly north-westwards. There are a couple more gates and a stile to cross to reach open country. Bear to the left to cross a nearby minor road at a point where there is a bridleway signpost.

The sign points along a stony track which runs gently downhill towards a building. Don't go all the way to the building, but turn left along a less clearly defined track and follow this uphill on a broad moorland slope. There are patches of bracken on the grassy moor in places. Follow the grooved track uphill, generally keeping to the left whenever there is a choice of directions. The idea is to follow the track uphill and gradually drift across the grassy crest to cut across the slopes of Loadpot Hill. The summit of Loadpot Hill stands at 2,201ft/671m and could be visited by making a short detour. For the purposes of this walk, however, follow the track cutting across the slopes and cross a boggy gap to link with a clear path on the course of the High Street Roman road.

Turn left to follow the path uphill, enjoying fine views on the ascent. The path reaches an upright stone set into a small cairn on Wether Hill and this is a good place to take in a panorama of fells.

Loadpot Hill's sprawling shape fills the northern prospect, while a portion of the Skiddaw and Blencathra fells can be seen. The Helvellyn range fills most of the view and gives way to the Fairfield group. A fine stretch of the North Pennines can also be seen.

There are no useful paths leaving the top of Wether Hill, and in mist it would be necessary to steer a course using a map and compass. In clear weather it is possible to look across to the broad, grassy crest of High Kop and pick a way towards it which doesn't run into peat hags and bog. The idea is to keep drifting leftwards and start descending along the crest. A number of paths will be seen ahead, drifting all over Low Kop. Keep to the right to follow a clear path across the slope overlooking Measand Beck. This path becomes quite good and passes a ruined building before making a sweeping zigzag down to a broad gap.

Climbing uphill from the gap, there are good views across Haweswater and the path remains firm and clear. There is a descent into a hollow filled with bracken, but the path cuts a clear swathe through it all to reach the farm of Drybarrows. Go through the gate into the farmyard, then keep to the right

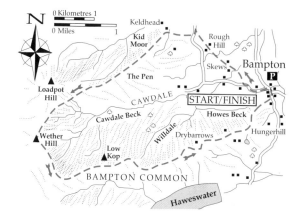

to pick up the course of a field path. This passes another farmhouse, then cuts across fields linking stone stiles with wooden step stiles. When a minor road is reached, turn right, then left at the next gateway. A track runs towards two gates. Go through the one on the right and pass a number of oak trees. The path crosses another stile and heads downhill towards a building. Pass the building on the right-hand side and then follow the line of a fence downhill towards Bampton.

HARTSOP

Walkers who travel beyond the head of Ullswater will find themselves in a quandary. There are a dozen fine fellwalks which could be attempted and each could be varied in significant ways. Standing near Hartsop and looking around at the fells which crowd the skyline causes the feet to shuffle impatiently. There are so many walks, so many ridge routes, so many little dales, so much to discover.

Only three routes are described in this section, narrowing the choice, but still revealing enough of the terrain to make it easy to spot opportunities for extensions and variations. One of the walks climbs from Brothers Water to the Kirkstone Pass Inn, then crosses Stony Cove Pike before descending from Threshthwaite Mouth to Hartsop. This route could easily be extended across the broad shoulders of High Street by keen fellwalkers.

A second route runs up through Dovedale from Brothers Water. This route creeps close to the overhanging Dove Crag, where the curious Priest's Hole could be inspected. After crossing over the top of Dove Crag the route heads for Scandale Pass to descend back to Brothers Water.

Moving a little down-dale from Hartsop, there is a third route which is based on Patterdale. This is like an alternative Fairfield Horseshoe route. Unlike the classic route from Ambleside, this route reveals more of the rough and rocky side of Fairfield and its neighbouring fells. St. Sunday Crag is crossed before Fairfield, and the route returns along the hummocky crest of Hartsop above How.

Although there are only the small villages of Hartsop and Patterdale, there are a number of farmhouse B&Bs in the area, as well as the Youth Hostel at Patterdale.There is a good range of accommodation including camp sites and hotels. Shopping opportunities are more limited, with one at the Brotherswater Hotel and another at Patterdale, but the range of goods stocked is impressive. There are more shops available at neighbouring Glenridding.

Throughout the year there is a bus service linking Penrith and Patterdale, taking in the length of Ullswater. In the summer there are buses from Patterdale, passing Hartsop and crossing the Kirkstone Pass to reach Windermere and Bowness.

Patterdale

D G Mather

27 Kirkstone and Hartsop

Hartsop is a charming little village in a splendid dale surrounded by many fine fells. There are immensely varied walks which can be enjoyed in the area. The one described here is a circuit which includes one of the smallest lakes in the Lake District, as well as the highest pub. Dales scenery gives way to rugged fell scenery as the walk progresses, while the lovely village of Hartsop is reserved until the end of the walk.

Distance:
9 miles/14.5km
Height gain:
2,000ft/610m
Walking time: 5 hours
Type of walk: Paths and

tracks in the dales and rugged fellwalking on top.
Start/Finish: Cow Bridge, near Hartsop. GR403134.

The Cow Bridge car park is fairly small and lies beside a popular road in a beautiful dale. Those walkers who can start early will be able to secure a space, while others will have to look elsewhere – possibly drastically restructuring the route. There is an information board at the car park outlining some of the features around the dale head.

Start the walk by following a broad and obvious track away from the car park, passing along a wooded shore of Brothers Water. Some say that this is the smallest of the lakes, while others dismiss it as no more than a flooded field!

The track runs past the imposing structure of Hartsop Hall, then there is a left turn to be made at the next building. As the fields around the dalehead are being crossed, keep to the left side of the prominent fell of High Hartsop Dodd and cross over Caiston Beck. The path gradually climbs uphill and judging by its evident engineering it must have been a substantial highway in its time. The main A592 road crossing Kirkstone Pass has subsequently been routed on a parallel course on the opposite side of the valley. Follow the path uphill across the rugged fellside until forced onto the Kirkstone Pass road. From that point, follow the road to the Kirkstone Pass Inn at the top of the road. This is the highest pub in the Lake District at 1,500ft/457m.

To continue the walk, there is a stile on the left just before reaching the inn. A path runs uphill towards St. Raven's Edge, where it drifts off to the left and follows a wall along a rugged ridge. The wall leads onto the broad and hummocky top of Stony Cove Pike. Some fellwalkers call it John Bell's Banner, while others call it Caudale Moor. The highest point is not easily determined even in clear weather, but stands at 2,502ft/763m.

Stony Cove Pike is flanked by higher and finer fells, and its broad shoulders obscure the surrounding dales. To improve the prospect from the fell, it is necessary to trudge around the summit area to bring a host of interesting features into view. The High Street range

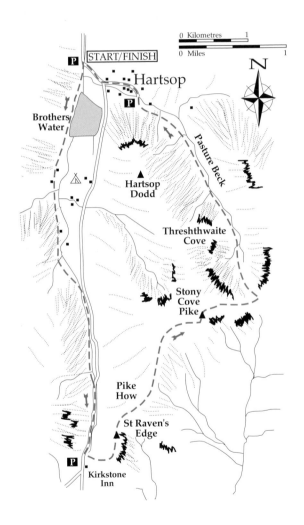

START/FINISH

Hartsop

Brothers
Water

Hartsop
Dodd

Pasture Beck

Threshthwaite
Cove

Stony Cove
Pike

Pike
How

St Raven's
Edge

Kirkstone
Inn

0 Kilometres 1

0 Miles 1

N

dominates all the way from the north, through east, to the south. Red Screes rises across the Kirkstone Pass, while the Scafells can be seen beyond it. The Helvellyn range fills the rest of the panorama.

There is a staggered wall junction near the top of Stony Cove Pike. By following the course of a ruined wall roughly eastwards a descent can be made to the rocky gap of Threshthwaite Mouth. Take care on this descent, as there is plenty of steep rock which can be greasy underfoot. On reaching the gap, turn left to drop steeply down the head of Threshthwaite Cove. There is a path which can be traced alongside Pasture Beck. As this proceeds, it moves away from the beck, crossing some boggy ground as well as negotiating a bouldery stretch of fellside. Don't cross over Pasture Beck until the wooded lower reaches of the dale are gained around Hartsop.

Cross over a bridge to reach Hartsop and spend a few moments admiring the many quaint old cottages in this tiny village. A narrow road runs straight through Hartsop and joins the main A592 road. Head straight along the main road to return to the Cow Bridge car park.

28 Dovedale and Dove Crag

Mention the names Dovedale and Dove Crag to most people and their minds will conjure up images of a snowy dove; a bird of peace; a promise of peace and contentment. In this instance the name is derived from the Celtic "dubh", meaning black. Dovedale is a dark dale; Dove Crag is a monstrous overhanging black crag, menacing and disturbing. Those who are looking for rugged, rocky surroundings will find it around Dovedale and Dove Crag. After the ascent, an easier fellwalk ends with a descent via Scandale Pass.

Distance: 8 miles/13km	steep and rugged climbing although with good paths throughout.
Height gain: 2,070ft/630m	**Start/Finish:** Cow Bridge, near Hartsop. GR403134.
Walking time: 5 hours	
Type of walk: Some	

Parking at the Cow Bridge car park can be difficult at peak periods, when the limited number of spaces are quickly occupied. Patrons of the Brotherswater Hotel or Sykeside campsite will be able to use the spaces provided at those places and complete a slightly shorter circuit. An information board on display at the car park includes a panorama of the fells around the dalehead and has interesting notes about the surrounding countryside.

Start the walk by following the broad and obvious track along a wooded shore of Brothers Water, continuing past the imposing structure of Hartsop Hall. After passing Hartsop Hall, continue as far as the outbuildings, where a small sign indicates a choice of routes into Dovedale.

To the left is a public footpath staying in the valley for a while longer, while to the right is a permitted fell path climbing uphill immediately. Take the latter path up the fellside, climbing through a pleasant woodland. Fine views from beyond the trees extend across the dale, while ahead the scene becomes crowded with crags.

The path running up through Dovedale is plain and obvious, having been originally constructed to serve a small quarry. There are views of delightful little waterfalls below, then the path turns more steeply uphill. A ruined building is passed, although it can be missed. If it is spotted, then have a look at its two rooms and note its fireplace, built-in slate shelf and cupboards.

A narrow scree path climbs steeply and care is needed on the loose stones. Above the scree the ferocious face of Dove Crag can be seen towering over the dalehead. Look carefully across the face to spot a natural cave in the crag, the Priest's Hole, which is used as a "bivvy" by hardy rock climbers.

It is possible to scramble up the rock and inspect the cave, but this is recommended only for those walkers with a good head for heights and the necessary keen balance. Walkers have only limited scope for exploring Dove

*Crag, which overhangs in places and proves to be wet
and greasy on closer acquaintance.*

Follow the path uphill to reach a gap, then turn left
and follow the course of a wall over the broad
summit of Dove Crag. The top bears a cairn at
2,603ft/792m. Most walkers crossing it will be
engaged on completing the Fairfield Horseshoe.

*As this is the highest point reached on the circuit around
Dovedale, the view can be studied for a while. Nearby
Fairfield and St. Sunday Crag block a view of the
Helvellyn range, but the whole of the High Street range
can be seen. There are glimpses of Coniston Water,
Windermere and Morecambe Bay to the south, with
parts of the Pennines featuring more distantly.*

Follow the fell wall roughly southwards from the
top of Dove Crag, then consider a couple of
options for the descent. A fence running off to the
left offers a faultless guide in mist over Little Hart
Crag and down to the top of Scandale Pass. In clear
weather, pass the fence and look out for another
path off to the left. This path has no guiding
feature, but is more interesting in good visibility. It
passes a group of cairns on a little hump called
High Bakestones and takes a more circuitous
fellside route to the Scandale Pass.

When the Scandale Pass is reached, follow the path
which runs roughly north-eastwards down
alongside Caiston Beck. The view down this
narrow dale widens to embrace Brothers Water
and eventually reaches the lower pastures. Follow
the path across the fields towards Hartsop Hall,

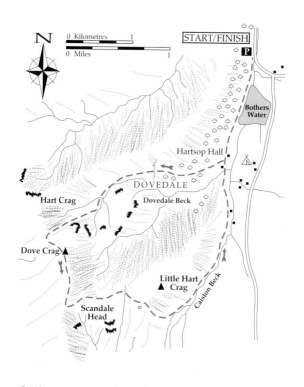

which was passed earlier in the day. All that remains is to retrace steps along the track passing Brothers Water to return to the Cow Bridge car park. Anyone heading for Sykeside or the Brotherswater Hotel can cut across the fields from Hartsop Hall.

29 St. Sunday Crag

St. Sunday Crag is an enormous wedge of fell between Grisedale and Deepdale. Its ascent can be tied in with neighbouring Fairfield, while the long ridge of Hartsop above How can be used to return to Patterdale afterwards. In effect, the route is like an alternative Fairfield Horseshoe, structured around Deepdale instead of Rydale. The route is altogether rougher than the Fairfield Horseshoe and takes in better views of the rugged gullies and buttresses on the northern slopes of Fairfield.

Distance: 10 miles/16km **Height gain:** 3,280ft/1,000m **Walking time:** 6 hours	**Type of walk:** Rugged fellwalking with some steep and rocky ridges. **Start/Finish:** Patterdale. GR394161.

It can be difficult to park around Patterdale, in which case the large car park at nearby Glenridding will have to be used. The walk starts by following the short minor road into Grisedale. There are sternly worded signs discouraging parking beside the road.

Walk along the road, passing the entrance to Home Farm, passing the next building, then taking a path left from the roadside. There is a little field to cross, then the path runs up a wooded slope in Glemara Park. Continue up through the woods to follow the path onto the rocky prow of Thornhow End. The path begins to drift to the right and is routed along a grassy strip above Birks Crag.

The ascent of the fell called Birks is an option on the way to St. Sunday Crag, but the clearest path merely cuts across the fellside in its rush towards greater things. The path gains more height by following a blunt ridge further uphill and there are splendid views back along the length of Ullswater. The path finally crosses the top of St. Sunday Crag, where there is a cairn perched at 2,756ft/841m.

Fairfield and the Helvellyn range can be studied in close-up detail, but they tend to block views of other fells. The exceptions are the Scafells and neighbouring groups seen through gaps in the range. The High Street fells are also seen from end to end.

The path leaving the top of St. Sunday Crag runs roughly south-westwards along a ridge which becomes narrower as the gap of Deepdale Hause is approached. Rising above Deepdale Hause is a rocky ridge which will require the use of hands for balance in a couple of places. Cofa Pike is a rugged boss of rock on the ridge, which can either be climbed or bypassed according to the whim of the walker. A final steep pull leads onto the broad, stony summit plateau of Fairfield. There are a host of cairns which prove confusing in mist, but there is also a large cairn marking the summit at 2,863ft/873m.

Views can be extensive, but it is often necessary to walk around the edge of the summit plateau to achieve a sense of depth and perspective. The additional height on

Fairfield means that other groups of fells move into view, extending either side of the Scafells previously noted. Looking southwards, Windermere and Coniston Water stretch towards the more distant Morecambe Bay.

Care is needed leaving the broad top of Fairfield in mist, as the multitude of cairns does not help with route finding. There is a path which eventually forms and leads towards the rugged hump of Hart Crag. In clear weather, however, it is worth picking a way along the top of the gullies and buttresses which fall from Fairfield's summit plateau. Either way, the cairn on top of Hart Crag is reached at 2,698ft/822m.

Leaving Hart Crag needs a little care. First walk a short way north-eastwards, then look carefully across the fellside to spot the path which threads its way downhill across steep and rocky terrain. Once this path has been located, there should be no other route finding problems. The slope eases later and a broad depression is reached on a blunt ridge. There are views down into Deepdale to the left and Dovedale to the right. A gentle climb along the line of the ridge leads to the summit of Hartsop above How. There is a chance to take a last look back at the craggy face of Fairfield and its neighbours before they pass from sight. Walkers engaged on the classic Fairfield Horseshoe route are quite unaware of the true nature of those crags.

Continue along the ridge of Hartsop above How. There is a long, but gentle, descent. Watch carefully for the line of the path on the lower, wooded slopes, and be sure to bear slightly to the left to drop down to Bridgend. Turn left to follow the A592 road back towards Patterdale from Bridgend. There are a couple of paths which have been constructed alongside the road to keep walkers away from the traffic, and it is recommended that these should be used.

GLENRIDDING

Glenridding can be a busy little village in the peak season, although many visitors seem quite happy just to potter around the village and the immediate shores of Ullswater. There are many who enjoy a short, easy walk without heading for the fells, but there are also those who set their sights high and are looking for more adventurous walks.

Striding Edge and Swirral Edge are greeted by different walkers in different ways. Some would not be drawn, while others would be eager to get to grips with the rock and go along those craggy edges to gain the summit of Helvellyn. The former may flick through this guide and pick an easier route over Helvellyn, while the latter may continue reading and sample the first walk in this section. Striding Edge and Swirral Edge may be popular, adventurous ridges, but they demand care and respect. In winter they are outside the scope of ordinary fellwalkers, and even in wet weather they can become slippery. The route is given for those who know they have the ability to complete it.

The second walk heads onto Sheffield Pike and proceeds around Green Side and Hart Side, crossing Glencoyne towards the end of the walk. There are likely to be a few walkers on these fells, but there won't be many. It is included for those walkers looking for a complete change of scenery.

An easy walk around Gowbarrow Fell is also offered. This concentrates on good paths and tracks, with a linking road stretch. There are intimate views of Aira Force, and lovely views along the length of Ullswater later.

Glenridding and Aira Force are regularly served by buses throughout the year. There is also a good range of accommodation at Glenridding and along the shore of Ullswater. Shops at Glenridding offer everything from food and drink to souvenirs and outdoor equipment. Aira Force features a tea room with snacks and refreshments. Walks over Hevellyn and Sheffield Pike could be extended by competent fellwalkers. There is scope to combine the two walks. Gowbarrow Fell is out on its own, with its nearest neighbours not really able to support good links of longer walks, but the little fell has charms all of its own.

Jean Marshall

Aira Force

30 Striding Edge and Swirral Edge

The most inspiring route on to Helvellyn is surely that which takes in Striding Edge and Swirral Edge – the two rocky ridges which embrace Red Tarn beneath the face of Helvellyn. Be warned that this route involves hands-on scrambling. In wet, windy or icy weather it could be very dangerous.

Distance: 8 miles/13km	*moderate fellwalking but*
Height gain:	*includes some steep and*
2,900ft/885m	*rocky ridges.*
Walking time: 5 hours	**Start/Finish:** *Patterdale.*
Type of walk: Mostly	*GR394161.*

Parking is restricted to a few small spaces around Patterdale and walkers who arrive too late to secure one of these will have to use the larger car park at nearby Glenridding, or that opposite the Patterdale Hotel.

The walk begins by following the short minor road into Grisedale. Follow the road to its end and turn right to drop down to Grisedale Beck. Cross the beck using a bridge, then climb straight uphill. The path later heads off to the left and cuts a broad and obvious line across the slopes of Birkhouse Moor. This is a popular path and there may already be legions of walkers crunching their way along it.

The path climbs to a celebrated landmark feature known as the "Hole in the Wall". This gap is readily spotted on the skyline in clear weather – and clear weather is really essential for the walk around Helvellyn's edges. The path proceeds beyond the wall and runs along the side of a blunt, rocky crest with a view of Red Tarn. The vast bulk of Helvellyn fills the scene ahead, and some walkers may be wondering where Striding Edge is supposed to be. The path climbs uphill and picks its way across increasingly rocky ground, then the edge gradually begins to become more and more apparent.

Take courage, as rock-climbing is not essential on Striding Edge. All that is needed is good weather, a good head for heights, and the occasional use of hands for balance.

At first, there is a good path pounded along the shattered rocky crest. Gaps in the ridge need a little care to cross and it is always better to watch where the feet are heading than to admire the waters of Red Tarn or the steep slopes plunging to either side of the ridge. There is a dramatic moment when it is possible to walk along the very crest of the ridge, although a few people prefer to cover this stretch on all fours.

Looking ahead, it becomes apparent that Striding Edge does not lead to the summit of Helvellyn. There is a deeper cleft in the rock and at this point walkers must use both hands and feet and gingerly pick a way down onto the gap. There is little point trying to outflank the crest of Striding Edge, as such moves often lead on to steep and unstable fellsides. From the gap, there is a steep and well worn braided path which continues uphill. The emergence onto the broad top of Helvellyn is sudden.

The first feature of note is a cross-shelter often filled with walkers enjoying lunch. Moving a little further uphill on pulverised gravel, the summit trig point on Helvellyn is gained at 3,118ft/950m. The extensive views encompass every notable range of fells in the Lake District, and there may well be a number of walkers rhyming off their names in all directions. More distant views stretch to the Pennines and southern Scotland. In very clear conditions it is possible to see all the way from The Cheviots to the mountains of Snowdonia.

Continuing around the edge of Helvellyn's summit from the trig point, another well worn path can be seen descending steeply to the right. This is the way off Helvellyn via Swirral Edge. Technically, Swirral Edge is easier than Striding Edge, but it still needs great care. The way downhill is steep and a sure footing is needed whenever gritty stones lie on top of bare rock. A slip on this path could be disastrous. Descending cautiously, the path eventually runs out onto a broad gap. Ahead is the pyramidal peak of Catstycam, which walkers should feel obliged to climb. An obvious path runs up to the summit at 2,917ft/890m. Enjoy the views, then follow the path back down to the gap.

There is a path leaving the gap and running down to the beck flowing from Red Tarn. Walk to Red Tarn, cross over the outflow and continue along the path contouring across the fellside in the

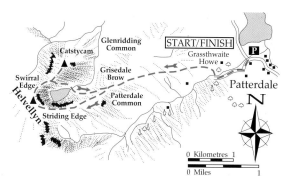

direction of Birkhouse Moor. The "Hole in the Wall" will be reached, where there may still be walkers making for Striding Edge and Helvellyn. All that remains is for steps to be retraced back down the fell to Grisedale and Patterdale.

31 Sheffield Pike

In their haste to climb Helvellyn many walkers completely overlook Sheffield Pike. It towers over Glenridding and those walkers who use the Sticks Pass as a line of ascent and descent pass fairly close to its summit. For the benefit of walkers who want to break from the pack, this route is offered which crosses Sheffield Pike and makes a fine circuit around the quiet dale of Glencoyne.

Distance: 6 miles/10km **Height gain:** 2,625ft/800m **Walking time:** 4 hours	**Type of walk:** A combination of rugged and easy fellwalking. **Start/Finish:** Glenridding. GR386169.

Glenridding can be a busy little village and walkers could be heading in all directions. There is a car park and information centre, shops and accommodation options, even a regular bus service and lake steamers.

Set off walking along the Greenside road to leave the village, climbing up to a row of fellside cottages. There is a stony and grassy path climbing straight uphill from the cottages, cutting a swathe across the brackeny fellside. Follow the path uphill and keep to the left to reach a gap between Sheffield Pike and Glenridding Dodd.

Turn left to follow a path up the rugged slopes of

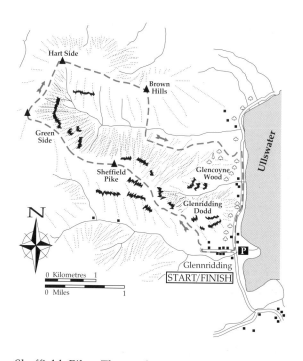

Sheffield Pike. The path twists and turns, side-stepping rocky outcrops on the steep slope. The gradient eases towards the top, and the ground features less rock. Some patches may be boggy and walkers should aim for a fine cairn on the summit at 2,232ft/675m.

Views should be enjoyed on the way to the summit, as they are not particularly good from the highest point. The Helvellyn and High Street ranges tend to dominate and neither groups are seen to their best advantage.

Descend westwards from the top of Sheffield Pike. A rugged patch quickly gives way to a grassier slope running down to a broad gap. Cross the gap and follow a grassy path up the next slope. The path passes the top of a great stony gash, then a beeline should be made for the broad top of Green Side. A couple of stony humps on this grassy fell bear cairns and the highest point rises to 2,610ft/796m.

The extra height above Sheffield Pike allows for a more extensive view, but the Helvellyn and High Street ranges still rule the skyline.

Walk roughly north-eastwards across a broad and grassy gap to reach the hump of Hart Side. This summit bears a curious trench and three cairns. Keep to the right and cross another grassy depression to reach a subsidiary summit of grass. Continue downhill from this point, heading towards a ruined wall. Cross over the wall and turn right to start following it downhill. The slope is steep, then it becomes steeper and rocky. Beware of a sudden drop on this descent, which can be outflanked by turning left, then right. The descent continues alongside a stouter wall. Pass a sheepfold and cross over Glencoyne Beck. Walk uphill a short way to reach a corner of the wall.

Turn left at the corner of the wall and follow a clear path. The path crosses bouldery ground as it follows the wall downhill. There is a stile at the edge of a woodland and the path runs downhill to land on a track near the cottage called Seldom Seen. Turn right and follow the track down to the

A592 road. Cross over the road and turn right to follow a path running between the road and the shore of Ullswater. The path later joins the road to get round a steep crag, then the path proceeds along the lake shore back to Glenridding.

32 Aira Force and Gowbarrow Fell

Rising uphill from the waterfalls is Gowbarrow Fell, a rugged and knobbly fell whose lower slopes are either divided into fields or planted with trees. Some walkers feel drawn to make a summit bid on Gowbarrow Fell. The walk described here is different, making a complete circuit around the lower and middle slopes of the fell without visiting the summit. Towards the end of the round there are some charming views across Ullswater.

Distance: 8 miles/13km	**Type of walk:** Generally an easy walk on paths, tracks and roads.
Height gain: 1,000ft/300m	**Start/Finish:** Aira Force.
Walking time: 4 hours	GR402201.

The National Trust provide good access to Aira Force, including a car park, toilets and tea room near the start.

Walk through the stone portal at the head of the car park and follow the path through two gates before entering a woodland. There is a network of paths around Aira Force, so the start of the walk could be varied. Go to the right, down a flight of steps, cross a footbridge, then follow more steps uphill. Bear to the left and follow a built-up path on a wooded slope, then go down and cross a stone footbridge.

There is a fine view of a slender waterfall plunging into a narrow, rocky gorge. Enjoy this spectacle for a while.

Follow a zigzagging flight of stone steps uphill and turn right at the top. Follow the path a short way and drop down to another stone footbridge. This spans the slender fall and gorge which were being observed only moments ago. Cross the bridge and turn left to follow a path upstream from Aira Force. There are a handful of smaller falls, but nothing as dramatic as those already seen. Keep to the path running fairly high above the beck, as those close to the banks tend to be more difficult, or peter out at obstacles.

Go through a little gate and emerge from the woods onto a field path. Continue the walk by following small blue signs for Ulcat Row. Keep to the path, noting a right turn before reaching a lovely cottage. Follow the next field path, continuing along a walled track, then using a farm track to reach a minor road at Ulcat Row. Turn right at the little hamlet to pass a chapel which has been converted into a dwelling. Follow the minor road onwards, down to cross Todgill Sike, then climbing before reaching a junction with another minor road. Turn right along the road for Watermillock. The road runs up to a gap called The Hause and there is a bench beside the road if any weary walkers need a rest. Cross the gap and follow the road downhill.

Look out for a small gate beside the road, marked as a footpath to Aira Force. A good track runs across a slope of bracken. It climbs as a narrower

path later and crosses a stile before running across the top of a forested slope. There are a couple more stiles to cross at the far edge of the forest around Swinburn's Park. A short, wooden walkway has been constructed across a steep slope, then the path mostly contours around a rugged fellside.

Follow the path around the face of Gowbarrow Fell which overlooks Ullswater and drink in the splendid views across the lake to the fells beyond. There is a cairn marking an excellent viewpoint, close to a stone seat which has been inscribed as "A Thank-Offering". After enjoying the fine view, follow the path downhill across the face of the fell. There is a stile to cross at a lower level, then steps run down to cross a bridge which was crossed earlier in the day. Follow the path up a flight of steps, out of the woods, and back towards the car park where the walk started.

MARTINDALE

Ullswater forms an effective barrier which keeps casual tourists away from Martindale. There is a narrow road leading into the area, passing only small settlements and scattered farmsteads. There are points along the road when fells seem to jostle for attention in the view, and a walker would feel inspired to start climbing them without delay. The layout of the higher fells is interesting, because there are summits arranged on a number of ridges separated by charming dales. There are several entertaining walks which could be completed by combining various ridges and dales on a series of long and short walks.

Three walks are offered in this section. The first route starts from Patterdale, crossing Place Fell and returning along a rugged and interesting lakeshore

A P Holt

Ullswater

path. This route allows a view into Martindale and a high vantage point from which to consider further plans. It is possible in the summer to use a ferry to reach Howtown and restructure the walk to start and finish at the landing pier.

The second route offers a fine circuit around Martindale, combining two of the delightful ridge walks with a walk on the higher fells. Again, there are vantage points from where the lie of the land can be studied, where the walker can take note of paths criss-crossing the fells. Loadpot Hill is a dome of a fell on sprawling moorland shoulders. It can be climbed from Martindale and is best reserved for a clear day.

There are a limited number of places offering accommodation, food and drink in Martindale, and most of the services are concentrated in nearby Pooley Bridge. Public transport is limited to two novel approaches. One is a Post Bus which operates throughout the year. Walkers thinking of using it are strongly advised to consult the timetable. In the summer, Martindale can be reached by the steamer service on Ullswater, either from Pooley Bridge or Patterdale. Motorists are obliged to use small parking spaces along the approach road.

33 Place Fell and Ullswater

Motorists on the road following Ullswater from Pooley Bridge to Patterdale can enjoy some fine views from time to time. Closer to Patterdale, those who look across the head of the lake are faced with an extremely rugged prospect. This is Place Fell, whose lumpy shoulders fill the sky and whose lower slopes fall straight into Ullswater. Climbing the fell is easier than it might first appear, and a circuit can be made by following a lakeshore path of exquisite beauty between Sandwick and Patterdale.

Distance: 8 miles/13km	fellwalking on good paths with an easy lakeshore path at the end.
Height gain: 2,130ft/650m	
Walking time: 5 hours	**Start/Finish:** Patterdale. GR394161.
Type of walk: Moderate	

There are only a few small parking spaces around Patterdale and any overflow is obliged to use the larger car park at neighbouring Glenridding, or that opposite the Patterdale Hotel. There is a climbing club hut beside the road at Patterdale, not far from St. Patrick's Church.

Just alongside the club building is a clear and obvious track which heads straight across the fields towards Side Farm. Follow the track to the farm, then turn right to trace an obvious path which slants diagonally across the fellside. This path is rough in places and generally runs in a deep groove, but it progresses uphill at a reasonable gradient towards Boredale Hause.

It isn't necessary to go quite to the top of the hause, as there is a path branching off to the left which starts climbing onto the upper slopes of Place Fell. The slope steepens a little, but not too much. There is outcropping rock, but nothing which obstructs progress. Simply follow the path as it zigzags uphill and at length the summit trig point will be gained at 2,154ft/657m.

Despite Place Fell having broad and knobbly shoulders, the summit is finely situated and offers an extensive view. The whole length of the Helvellyn range can be studied in detail, while Skiddaw and Blencathra also make an appearance. Southern Scotland and the North Pennines can be seen in clear weather beyond the Vale of Eden. The nearby High Street range occupies the rest of the panorama.

After sampling the vista, follow a path roughly north-eastwards away from the summit. This passes a pool of water, then runs down towards the subsidiary summit of High Dodd. Go straight through an intersection of paths and follow the path which cuts across the western slopes of Sleet Fell. Don't be tempted into the lower fields, but follow the fell wall which contours below Cat Crag. Follow the path down towards the hamlet of Sandwick when it comes into view.

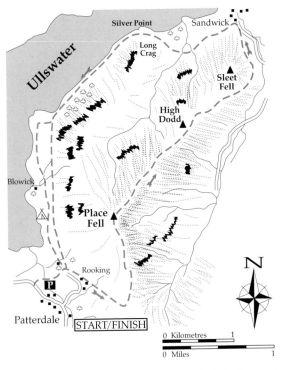

Silver Point

Sandwick

Ullswater

Long
Crag

Sleet
Fell

High
Dodd

Blowick

Place
Fell

Rooking

P

Patterdale

START/FINISH

N

0 Kilometres 1

0 Miles 1

There is no need to go into Sandwick. Instead, keep to the left and pick up the clear path which crosses a rugged, wooded fellside and takes in views of Scalehow Force. Further along, this path runs along a lovely stretch of Ullswater's shore, then turns around the rocky promontory of Silver Point. There are two alternative paths here, one staying low and one climbing higher over a rugged little gap. Whichever path is taken, they both join together further along. Masses of juniper and stunted trees cling to the rugged slopes of Place Fell, changing colouring through the seasons. The lakeshore path returns to Side Farm, where a right turn reveals the track running across the fields to return to Patterdale.

There are some walkers who enjoy the lakeshore walk from Patterdale to Howtown and return to Patterdale using the lake steamer service. This approach uses the most charming part of the walk and is an option to consider for those who cannot contemplate the walk over the top of Place Fell.

34 Martindale Horseshoe

Martindale is often considered to be off the beaten track, even though it lies just across Ullswater from some very popular places. The lake proves to be a barrier on one side, while the whole dale is surrounded by tall fells which guard it on all other sides. The fells offer the chance to complete an extended horseshoe walk, taking in the summits around Bannerdale and Rampsgill. In the middle of the walk is a deer forest, where herds of deer might be spotted as the walk progresses.

Distance:
11 miles/18km
Height gain:
2,950ft/900m
Walking time: 7 hours
Type of walk: Moderate
fellwalking but covering some distance and several summits.
Start/Finish: St. Martin's Church, Martindale. GR434184.

The old church of St. Martin's sits low against the fellside beside a dead-end road in an out-of-the-way dale. Have a look inside and explore the churchyard before starting the walk.

A path rises steeply behind the church and bears to the right as it climbs diagonally across the fellside. The line of the path across the slopes of Steel Knotts is obvious, but it misses the pointed rock summit of Pikeawassa in its eagerness to reach the higher fells. The path runs along the ridge of the fell and becomes rather vague near a wall on Gowk Hill. Look carefully and the path re-establishes itself as a fine track up the flank of Wether Hill.

The last part of the climb reaches the corner of a fence. Turn right at this point and follow the fence roughly southwards. This is the approximate course of an old Roman road known as High Street, which was blazed all the way across the tops of the High Street fells. There is a path running close to the fence which becomes more and more well trodden. It runs across a broad moorland close to the stony summit of High Raise, which peaks at 2,634ft/802m.

This is the highest point gained on the walk and it offers the most extensive panorama. The High Street and Helvellyn ranges dominate much of the view, but there are glimpses of more distant fells beyond them. The North Pennines and Howgills also feature across the Vale of Eden.

Continue straight beyond High Raise, towards the broad rise of Rampsgill Head. It is important to take care over route finding on this stretch in mist. Don't drift left onto Kidsty Pike, but keep more to the right and look out for a prominent wall. Turn right to follow the wall, which has an accompanying path running downhill. Pass the minor bump called The Knott and continue downhill.

There are two options: one is to keep to the path, which cuts across the flanks of Rest Dodd; the

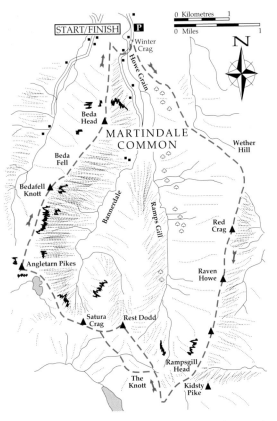

other is to follow the wall, which leads up the slopes of Rest Dodd. It's worth including Rest Dodd's summit as it offers a fine view around Martindale. The wall doesn't run all the way to the summit, so branch away from it to reach the cairn at 2,278ft/697m. Enjoy the view around the dales and fells, also trying to spot deer on The Nab.

Descend westwards to pick up the line of the path again on Satura Crag. The terrain is rocky and hummocky, but the path threads a way through it and skirts around the strangely shaped Angle Tarn. Leave the path and head straight uphill to gain the top of Angletarn Pikes. Look ahead to try and spot a path running roughly northwards along a hummocky crest connecting Angletarn Pikes with Beda Fell. The ridge path is fairly clear and conveys walkers to an intersection with another path on Bedafell Knott. Ailing walkers could exit to the right at this point and reach the low ground early.

Staying high on Beda Fell is preferred. There is little climbing along the ridge to the summit, which rises to an altitude of 1,664ft/509m. As this fell is fairly central to the Martindale fells, there is a chance to have one last good look around. The whole of the route can be traced from this stance, and more distant features can be spotted despite the crowding of nearby, higher fells.

Continue northwards along the ridge of Beda Fell. The path is deceptive and appears to run all the way to Hallin Fell, as if that fell were also on the same ridge. At a much lower level, almost at the end of the ridge, a path crosses over from Boardale to Martindale. Turn right to follow the path down into Martindale, then walk a short stretch of road to return to the old church of St. Martin's.

35 Loadpot Hill

Loadpot Hill is a broad and sprawling moorland towards the northern end of the High Street range. An ascent can be combined with the more shapely ridge of Steel Knotts, with its pointed summit of rock. A descent can be made on the rugged slopes of Bonscale Pike, so that a circuit could be made from near Howtown. In this area, Hallin Fell constantly beckons walkers to make a summit bid. It rises just above the road at St. Peter's Church and dips its feet in Ullswater, promising extensive lake views.

Distance:
8 miles/13km
Height gain:
2,430ft/740m
Walking time: 5 hours
Type of walk: Moderate

fellwalking with care needed in mist on the broader tops.
Start/Finish: *St. Peter's Church, Martindale.* GR435192.

St. Peter's Church sits on The Hause between Howtown and Martindale. There is parking for a few cars on the gap, and it is worth having a look in and around the church before starting the walk. St. Peter's was built to replace the old church of St. Martin's nearby, but somehow the old church remains in use.

The walk can begin behind the church, picking up a path which climbs uphill on the northern slopes of Steel Knotts. The short and steep climb later becomes easier and there should be no problem following the ridge of the fell.

The summit is a spike of rock called Pikeawassa, rising to 1,414ft/433m. Despite its small stature, the view is exceedingly good, although somewhat one-sided. Hallin Fell causes Ullswater to appear twice in the view, while the bulky Place Fell obscures Helvellyn, although other parts of the range can be seen. The nearby views over Martindale are especially charming.

Continue along the ridge path, although it does become a little obscure further along. Beyond Gowk Hill there is a clearer track running up onto the slopes of Wether Hill. Turn left when the broad moorland crest is reached and follow a path over the dull rise of Wether Hill. The path is roughly the course once blazed by the Roman road known as High Street. There is a bit of a depression in the moorland crest before a gentle climb up the slopes of Loadpot Hill. The crumbled ruins of a former shooting hut are passed on a direct ascent towards the summit. In mist, be careful not to be drawn either right or left along paths which miss the summit.

The top of Loadpot Hill is an undistinguished area of moorland with a small cairn at 2,201ft/671m. The broadness of the summit makes views less attractive, and in any case other fells seem rather remote. The Helvellyn and Skiddaw fells take up much of the view, and only part of the High Street range can be seen. There is an uninterrupted view towards the North Pennines and in clear weather parts of southern Scotland may be seen.

Walk roughly northwards off the top of Loadpot Hill. Ahead is a rolling moorland apparently devoid of interest. The only prominent path is a

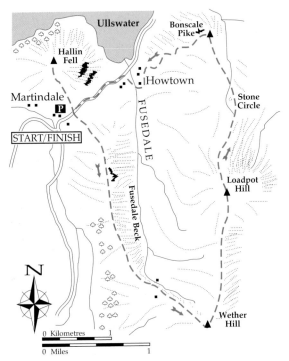

groove in the moorland, and it is important not to be drawn along it in mist, as it runs practically all the way to Pooley Bridge. Instead, cross over the groove and look carefully to spot a small stone circle, one of a handful which can be distinguished around Loadpot Hill.

In clear weather, the only features to be seen ahead are a couple of prominent cairns on Bonscale Pike. Neither of these stands on a high point, but both overlook Ullswater and offer fine views.

Having reached a rocky edge on Bonscale Pike, perhaps the safest thing to do is to walk a short distance southwards, then look down the flanks of the fell to spot the line of an old path. There is a way down the steep, rugged, brackeny fellside using the sweeping zigzags described by the old path. Aim to reach the fellside wall at Mellguards and head for the prominent Howtown Hotel beyond. After passing the Hotel, or stopping for a break as the case may be, turn left along the winding minor road which runs back up to St. Peter's Church on The Hause.

The walk can end at St. Peter's, or if energy levels allow, then a short extension can be enjoyed. Hallin Fell rises opposite St. Peter's and for many casual strollers this is reckoned to be an easy fell to climb. A broad grassy path makes a beeline for the summit, which is crowned by a stout, square cairn of monumental proportions.

As a bonus, the view is marvellous, extending along the levels of Ullswater and taking in most of the Helvellyn range. The Martindale and High Street fells also feature well.

Simply retrace steps to return to St. Peter's. Avoid the temptation to descend towards the Ullswater shore as there are some very rough and rocky slopes in that direction.

FURTHER READING

Lakeland Villages, Jim Watson, (Cicerone Press).

Lakeland Towns, Jim Watson, (Cicerone Press).

A Dream of Eden, John Dawson, (Cicerone Press).

Companion Guide to the Lake District, Frank Welsh, (Collins).

The Lakeland Peaks, Walter Poucher, (Constable).

Lake District Landscape Heritage, William Rollinson (ed), (David & Charles).

50 Best Scrambles in the Lake District, Bill O'Connor, (David & Charles).

The Naturalist in Lakeland, Eric Hardy, (David & Charles).

A Pictorial Guide to the Lakeland Fells – Northern, Eastern & Far Eastern Fells, A Wainwright, (Michael Joseph).

The Outlying Fells of Lakeland, A Wainwright, (Michael Joseph).

The Lakers, Norman Nicholson, (Robert Hale and Cicerone Press).

Numerous leaflets and booklets can be obtained from Tourist Information Centres.

Other Dalesman titles for walkers

Walking and Trail Guides

LAKE DISTRICT, WESTERN FELLS
Paddy Dillon £5.99
WHITE PEAK Martin Smith £4.99
DARK PEAK John Gillham £4.99
NORTH PENNINES Alan Hall £4.99
SOUTH PENNINES John Gillham £4.99
CLEVELAND WAY Martin Collins £4.99
PENNINE WAY Terry Marsh £4.99

Walks Around Series: Peak District

BAKEWELL Martin Smith £1.99
BUXTON Andrew McCloy £1.99
CASTLETON John Gillham £1.99
MATLOCK Martin Smith £1.99

Walks Around Series: Lake District

AMBLESIDE Tom Bowker £1.99
HAWKSHEAD Mary Welsh £1.99
KESWICK Dawn Gibson £1.99
WINDERMERE Robert Gambles £1.99

Pub and Tea Shop Walks Series

LAKE DISTRICT Terry Marsh £5.99
NORTH YORK MOORS & COAST
Richard Musgrave £5.99